Don't be a **D.U.M.B.** Business Owner

619.688.9248
thrivebusinessservices.net

Mike Milan

ISBN: 978-1-952263-77-4

Dedication

For the small business owner who avoids being D.U.M.B. while building a lifestyle-friendly business for themselves and their family.

Acknowledgment

Man, this is a trip. Who would have ever thought I would finally write the book I talked about for years, I guess all it took was the love and encouragement of the most important woman in my life, Courtney. Not only did she give me not so gentle nudges in this direction, but she also sat through dozens of live seminars, and even came up with the name of my signature program, The Clear Path to Cash. For all of this, I am grateful. I love you.

The content of this book is a culmination of past experiences and the introduction to a dynamic teaching style, where you not only make complex ideas easy to understand, you bring boring material to life. I was inspired by Kyle, and his father Dave, who are Masters of Financial Management and icons in the banking industry.

With that in mind, I would never have had the chance to stand in front of an audience full of bankers, accountants, and business owners, without James taking a chance on hiring me at a financial technology company with no software experience.

Lastly, I want to acknowledge my biggest fan, Shane In the earliest days of my training programs, he downloaded and listened to every one of them, even the one I did live in Nashville. His confidence in me, gave me the motivation to continue to work on this craft and be able to write this book.

Each of you made this dream of mine possible. Thank you.

About the Author

Cash Flow Mike

Cash Flow Mike is addicted to starting new business ventures. His resume is super messy, probably worse than yours. Here is a short list of stuff he has done.

- Spent 16 Years in the Army National Guard and 7 Years as a Missouri State Trooper
- Built a 500-employee hotel staffing firm
- Owned and operated 3 bar/restaurants
- Owned and managed numerous pieces of rental property
- Failed at an herbal supplement company after getting the product in 119 Walgreen stores
- Ran a construction team for a large non-profit

- Built a financial software application for small businesses and accountants
- Trained 1000's of bankers, accountants & business owners on the art of financial management
- Created the Clear Path To Cash blueprint strategy
- Wrote two books: Don't Be D.U.M.B. Business Owner & The 7 Minute Conversation
- Earned MBA from Baylor University
- Has Three awesome & beautiful daughters
- Is a Motorcycle and Golf Enthusiast
- Jumped from airplanes, wrote poetry, & fell in love

Preface

I lost ten years of my life. Yes, ten years. Lost might be a harsh term, but honestly, I just didn't see it happen. Ten years had come and gone before I could stop to think about what I had done. I had lived the "average" entrepreneur's dream and now lived to tell the story. At the time, it was chaos and bliss. I laughed and cried. I made mistakes and executed a few phenomenal successes. I wouldn't trade a day of the last ten years.

The nagging question I had was why did it have to be so hard? Why did I have weeks/months where I didn't get a paycheck, so I could pay everyone else? I agonized over cash flow and even changed my business strategy completely to alleviate some of the pressure. I never felt like I was a D.U.M.B. business owner, but I was only kidding myself. Here is what I realized. My "trusted advisors" just talked over my head. I didn't understand half of what they said, especially when they used words like solvency and leverage.

They just talked at an entirely different level of financial sophistication and I didn't "get it. Over the years, I found out that I wasn't alone. It was like all the cool kids had learned a secret language and if you didn't know it – too bad. The result was a struggling business, something that happens to almost 1 million businesses per year.

I set about trying to educate myself, I even went back to school and earned an MBA. I learned the meaning of the fancy words my advisers and professors used, but I found out even more about the world of business. I found out, that the biggest failure in the adviser/owner relationship wasn't the lack of comprehension of the business owner. It was the inability of the adviser to explain it at the business owners' level. In fact, I was surprised to find out that my adviser, couldn't simplify any of the financial concepts he talked about without using the words most people don't understand. For example, he would say:

"An improvement in leverage suggests an improvement in long-term solvency, while an improvement in liquidity is a good signal about your company's ability to service your current debt obligations."

WHAT?

Why not just say this?

"If you pay down your equipment loan, you can stay in business longer, but if we can get some more cash into the business now, we can make sure you can make your credit card payment this month."

Just talk to me the way I talk normally. I wouldn't need an MBA to decipher the secret code.

This is what inspired me to create the Clear Path to Cash. It is an 8 Step training program for the average business owner and their advisory team to execute. The program itself is designed to maximize cash in any given business situation, but more importantly, it creates a simple to understand the connection between ratio analysis and the real-world.

If you're anything like me, then this book will accelerate your understanding of the complex financial concepts that most highly educated are trained to evaluate. The good thing is that you don't have to spend $50k like I did to learn it.

I thank you for taking the first step in creating a lifestyle-friendly business for you and your family. Your business is a huge investment and a wonderful mechanism to create wealth. Before you know it; you will be on the Clear Path to Cash.

Best wishes for success,

The Clear Path to Cash

1. Start with The End in Mind
2. The Home Run Financial System
3. Mining Your Business for Hidden Cash
4. The Fast Money Formula
5. Forecasting by The Numbers
6. How to Deal with Your Bank
7. The Simple Valuation Formula
8. The Deliberate Exit Strategy

Contents

dedication .... *i*
Acknowledgment ....*ii*
About The Author..*iv*
Preface ....*vi*

Chapter 1- Start With The End In Mind................................ *1*
Chapter 2- What's It Worth To You *14*
Chapter 3- The Home Run Financial System *23*
Chapter 4- Find Hidden Cash With This Method............... *53*
Chapter 5- Test.. *63*
Chapter 6- Analyze.. *93*
Chapter 7- Diagnose *114*
Chapter 8- Treat... *130*
Chapter 9- The Fast Money Formula *151*
Chapter 10- Forecasting By The Numbers - A Step By Step Guide *177*
Chapter 11- How To Deal With Your Banker *207*
Chapter 12- The Simple Business Valuation Formula *225*
Chapter 13- The Deliberate Exit Strategy *250*
Chapter 14- So, What's The Point?................................. *269*

Page Left Blank Intentionally

Chapter 1
START WITH THE END IN MIND

Whether you're running a business or planning to run one, what do you think is the chief purpose of your business?

Well, your answer may differ from mine. However, according to my experience and observation, a majority of people start a business because they want to earn money. In fact, we all want that. Who doesn't dream of a fulfilling lifestyle? There is nothing wrong with running a business for making money. However, the approach we adopt is what makes our business success or failure. Making money is a result, and results can only be achieved through effective planning. Therefore, the main goal of a business should be to be successful, and then money will follow automatically. Remember, small businesses love order. They thrive in a process-driven environment, where every part contributes to the creation of a result. Since business is an economic entity, results are usually measured in dollars. A business with poor or misguided order generates poor results. Our goal is to create an orderly process that produces the highest amount of dollars while simultaneously satisfying our reason for doing it.

After establishing eight businesses in the last 16 years, acquiring an MBA, and consulting several hundred other small businesses, I realized that businesses were tamable. A small business gravitates towards order, either the one you create or the one your customers and employees create. Preferably, the one you create. If not, disaster could strike, and your life will get messy real fast. It happened to me.

It's not that I'm unintelligent, it's just that I got distracted. I was wrapped up in thousands of details that made up my daily business life. However, I completely neglected the results my business was generating. I got caught up in the day-to-day tasks of running my business, without knowing if I was successful or not. I felt busy. I felt important. I just didn't feel satisfied with progressing towards my dream of being financially comfortable. I had what others considered as a great business, but when it came to the true purpose of my business; I was D.U.M.B.

I **D**idn't **U**nderstand **M**y **B**usiness. Not true anymore though. I wasn't able to get a firm grip on my business objectives until later on.

When you become D.U.M.B, you lack or lose control over your business. In most cases, during the initial stages of the business journey, it is extremely difficult to remove your doubts and stay focused on a specific goal. As a result, you or any other aspiring entrepreneur are unable to channel their energies effectively. I can say this with such surety because I was sucked into a stream of unnecessary distractions. Consequentially, I became too fixated on the intricate details of my business operations and processes. This fixation didn't allow me to pay attention to the results I was getting, and, because of that, I made mistakes and lost money. Once your business has escaped your control, it takes a lot of work to get it back. Trust me, I have lived through turnarounds, and they are complex and demanding. However, this hard work is worth it.

Don't worry, I won't keep how to get back on track a secret and throughout this book, you will come across a plethora of techniques and hidden facts that successful professionals and business owners never reveal.

When you move through the "fog" of a chaotic business, the reward is a clear view of a healthy business that generates transferrable value. Additionally, a business under your control just needs small adjustments to stay on course.

My purpose of writing this book is to help my readers "tame the beast" by sharing some lessons I have learned in my life. It starts with understanding your business and the "levers" you have as an owner. Levers that control the direction of the company and move it in the direction you intend to. Quite simply, running a small business begins with "taming" the beast and building a machine – a cash machine to be exact.

You obviously don't want to be a D.U.M.B. business owner, I mean, nobody does. If you want to know the traits of a D.U.M.B business owner, you can easily identify these individuals from their stories and background. You may have come across the people who describe how their successful business ran out of money or failed because the market soured. They are the ones who you can call as D.U.M.B because they always blame the results of their actions on external factors. Running a business can be like learning to ride a horse. It is a little scary at first, but with a few maneuvers and time, it can be second nature.

Spending your working life doing something that inspires you is one thing but building an asset that supports your lifestyle beyond your working years is another. Our ultimate goal is to build transferrable value. Transferable value is the amount of money you need to do whatever it is you want to do the next. The sooner you put this dollar amount as the focal point of your decisions, the easier it will be to achieve. This is starting with the end in mind.

Transferable Value

It all starts with your decision about what your future looks like. Once you have an idea of what you are spending your time, money, and energy working toward, a clear path to getting there starts to emerge. Understanding what transferable value is and then calculating how much transferable value you need to create is Step 1 in The Clear Path to Cash.

When we think of value in terms of finance, different terms pop up in our minds, such as fair market value, intrinsic value, or book value. However, transferable value is different from all of them. Transferable value is simply the worth of your business without YOU. Or in simple words, it is the value of your business to a new buyer without you in it. More importantly, you can transfer the cash value generated by the business to your personal accounts throughout the life of the business.

Let's look at it this way. Imagine there are three companies. They all are renowned companies with an EBIT (Earnings before interest and taxes) of $3.5 million and $40 million in annual revenue. Now apparently, it seems that three businesses are of equal worth. However, this is not the case. When these companies are sold, all of them will be sold at totally different values.

Do you know why?

Because of the difference in their value drivers.

The internal characteristics of a business are called its value drivers. Strong Value Drivers are the important attributes that will continue to exist even if the original owner departs. These drivers include shareholder value, suppliers, management, customer base, competitive advantage, and so forth. If the value drivers are effective, then, in that case, the company's revenue and EBIT keep increasing regardless of who the owner is.

When a company is available for acquisition, the potential buyers will be looking at its value drivers. Let's face it, nobody wants to pay a premium for your problems. The more effective and efficient your people and processes are, the more valuable your company will be.

We calculate the efficacy of value drivers by their ability to contribute to cash flow under new ownership. Transferable value signifies that the success of your business is not only defined by how well you run it, but also by how efficiently it runs without your presence.

The above description was from a potential buyer's perspective. When we talk about it from an owner's outlook, it starts with answering a simple question. That question is

"Do I have enough money to do whatever I want to do when I leave this company behind?"

If the answer is yes, then you have built transferrable value. If the answer is no, you have built yourself a job.

Transferrable value means something different to each of us.

One owner may want to travel the world when they are done working, while another might be satisfied with watching sunsets in the Hill Country of Texas. The point being, that the amount of money it takes to fund either of those dreams will be different. Transferable value is an individual pursuit. A pursuit you can't leave to chance.

How Do You Get the Most Out of Your Small Business?

"Run it like you're selling it."

Have you ever placed a car you own up for sale?

What is the first thing you do?

You clean it up, right? Then you fix the things that need to be fixed. You get the leftover pizza and fries out from between the seats. You get the car ready to present to someone else in the hopes that it will attract top dollar. It's natural for us to do this. We are trying to get the most out of anything we want to sell.

An interesting thing happens right after you clean up your old vehicle, especially, if you are still driving it daily. As you get behind the wheel, you are amazed by the way it drives. It's so smooth, it looks better, and it even smells better. You have flashbacks of how happy you were with this car when you first bought it.

You even start to think, *"This is a pretty nice car."* All of the issues that made you ready to sell have suddenly disappeared. What a bonus! Then what made it so nice and enjoyable now?

You get the benefit of riding in a "pretty nice car" throughout the entire period that it sits on the market. You later get an offer that is good and beyond your expectations. The buyer gets the same feeling of having a "pretty nice car."

The point of presenting all this analogy is to run your small business like you're trying to sell it, even if you have no current plans to put it on the market. Much like putting a car on the market, your business will feel the same way. You will feel a new energy in your business, and so you will start reaping the benefit of the cash a healthy business produces. If you want to attract top dollar from a buyer when you intend to sell, show them that your business is clean and well maintained.

When I say clean, I literally mean clean. First impressions are critical in getting a buyer to look a little closer at your operation. If you have been in business for a while, you might look around your business and see little messes that have accumulated. Clean up projects that you set aside as a low priority, as they can clutter the workspace.

In a recent consulting engagement, an area needing immediate attention was the indoor/outdoor warehouse. When I pulled up to the front door of the business, I parked in a gravel lot surrounded by piles of seemingly unorganized items. Not small piles, but ones taller than my vehicle and looking like the heaps you would imagine to be in a junkyard. To a potential buyer, this first impression is one that screams, *"This business needs a lot of work."*

Take the time to clean up the little messes that have accumulated around your workplace. You might be surprised to find that the mood of the workforce will improve, leading to a boost in productivity. People love to work in a clean environment. It is one that they can be proud of and feel good about driving to each morning. It could be a big task upfront but easily maintained after you get it done. Make this your first priority, just like you would wash and clean your vehicle.

The second and possibly more difficult task is to fix the issues that are contributing to your operation being less than optimal. If you don't know where to start, start by comparing your financial operation to those of companies in a similar industry. Your goal is to operate better than the average company. Look specifically at how much gross and net profit they have compared to yours. This is the report card for how efficient your operation is. Potential buyers like to buy the cash flow your company is producing without a lot of effort. This is a similar goal of the person wanting to buy your used car. They want the immediate satisfaction of driving the car without the effort of having to fix it.

Once you spiff up your business, you get the immediate benefit that any buyer would have. You benefit from the profit and cash the business produces every year before you decide to sell. Once the company is generating cash, the disciplined business owner will set some aside to fund their vision of the future, their transferable value amount.

Once you decide to sell, a buyer will reward you again with an above-the-market offer. Why?

Because buyers love to acquire companies that can instantly provide them with value. The better your company operates, the lower the risk a potential buyer has. Whether it's your business or your used car, buyers just want to jump in the driver's seat and go. Make it easy for them to take the wheel and you will both be happy.

Selling your company is just one option you have to help fund your future. I say it should be the main source of funding if you have the opportunity to start working towards it today. You can't wait. The longer you wait, the fewer the options you will have to achieve your goal. I don't want you to have to change your dream or lower your expectations. Starting with the end in mind, helps you focus on the result today and make smaller incremental decisions to fill your transferable value account.

Chapter 2
WHAT'S IT WORTH TO YOU

How is Transferable Value Important for a Financial Advisor?

It's natural that when you start a journey you would have a destination set in mind. Starting or running a business is no different. You must know where your clients are wanting to go. This entails working with your clients to understand two things about their business.

1. What are they working for? What is their dream that they are investing in everything for?

2. What does it cost to fund their dream? Money is never the final dream. They need money to do something else.

Transferable value isn't something that accountants and their clients regularly talk about, in fact, maybe never. But transferable value is the destination in your business ownership journey. Transferable value is simply the amount of money the business owner wants to have, whenever they decide to do something different. If you are going to help your clients achieve their goal, start here, with the end in mind. The concept is the same for small business owners and their advisers alike.

Here's an example: Your clients are a couple around 30-years-old. They have a plan to retire at the age of 50. Moreover, they expect that they will live for another 25 years. Most people live approximately 25 years after they quit working. So, it's prudent to use this timeframe to plan your future. When they retire, they want to have an annual payment of $100,000 till they die (i.e. for 25 years after they retire). Now, they want to start saving money beginning today.

With just this little bit of information, we know that they will need approximately $2.5 million to fund their idea of what retirement will look like. ($100,000 per year * 25 years = $2.5 million). For those of you that swim in the deep end of the financial knowledge pool, don't freak out here. We are keeping this calculation simple on purpose so everyone can plan for their future.

Here is some other information to help us determine how much money this couple will need to set aside each year to reach their goal. The market interest rate they think they can realistically get by investing is 5%. They currently have $200,000 in savings.

After learning about your clients' goals and their level of commitment, you are ready to start putting a value on their dream. Use the facts you learned above to calculate an annual cash requirement to fund their transferable value. You can find a downloadable spreadsheet to calculate this number for them quickly at this website: www.clearpathtocash.com. This calculation is considered as Step 1 in The Clear Path to Cash Strategy.

What we need to know about your client:

Time Period (n): 20 years (they are 30 now and want to retire at 50 years old)

Interest rate (r): 5%

PV (Present Value): $200,000

FV (Future Value -Transferable Value): $2,500,000

This information now becomes the basis for all your future conversations with your clients. Now, let's put our first reality check on our clients' information to get a sense of how likely it is our clients can achieve their goal.

Figure 2.1

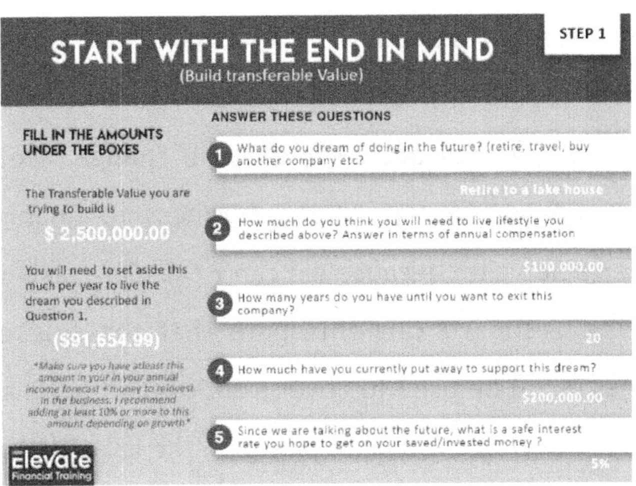

Using the PMT formula in excel your clients will need to save or set aside $91,654.99 per year in order to save $2.5 million by the time they are 50 years old. Here is the formula for excel if you would like to do it yourself, or you can download my spreadsheet at www.cashflowmike.com. The first question we should ask is if this number is doable. This may be the first time that your client has seen the amount they should be contributing. Based on the size of the business, this number might be easy or impossible to achieve. In either case, we now have a number to build your business forecast against.

You may also notice that I did not include the value of the business in this calculation. That is because we assume that the couple will continue to own and operate the company until they decide to make a change. We don't want to rely on a sale of the business to finance our transferrable value because we can't calculate its worth in 20 years. Also, we can anticipate that the sale of the business might be used to cover a shortfall in our planning or choose to view the sale as "icing on the cake".

Bottom line: Do not rely on the value of your company to finance your future unless you have to.

Similarly, we can take the case of a John, a 50-year-old owner of a plumbing company, who is just ten years away from his retirement. John wishes to live in Hidden Hills, a Los Angeles, a gated community in the next 10 years so that he can retire in peace with headaches of maintaining a home on his own. He has a total of $450,000 that he has been able to save over his lifetime. Based on his estimates, he believes he will need about $75,000 per year to live in the community the way he wants to.

Based on our way to calculate the transferable value, John would need $1,875,000 to live in Hidden Hills during retirement. A few things are working against John in this scenario. Time being the biggest. He only has 10 years to accumulate enough funds to fund his dream. Additionally, he has only accumulated $450,000 to this point. This means that he will have to save an additional $196,493.56 per year for the next 10 years. OUCH.

Here are the calculations assuming he can achieve 8% interest:

Figure 2.2

ANNUAL INTEREST RATE EARNED	TERM IN YEARS	PRESENT VALUE	FUTURE VALUE	PAYMENT TO TRANSFERABLE VALUE	FORMULA
8%	10	$450,000.00	$ 1,875,000.00	($196,493.56)	"=PMT(A4,B4,C4,D4

Using the "Forecasting by The Numbers" spreadsheet, the result would look like this:

***F*igure 2.3**

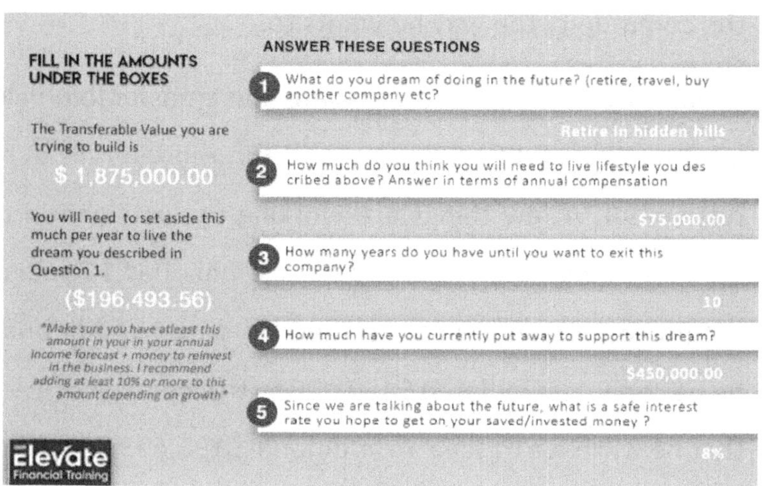

Chance is that John won't be able to generate $196,493 per year in his plumbing company to fund his retirement dream. This is when reality sets in. John basically has three options:

1. **Set aside as much as he can each year until retirement and adjust his retirement lifestyle to match the amount of money he can accumulate.**
2. **Get lucky and save as much as he can and hope he can sell his company for enough money to make up the**

difference in what he can save and what he needs to live in Hidden Hills.

3. **Do nothing and figure it out later.**

In any case, by waiting so long, John has limited his realistic options for retirement. We don't want this to happen to you, nor do we want you to depend on "hope" to achieve your dream.

As a capable financial advisor, you must ask your client whether this number is manageable for them in the early stages of your business relationship. If you fail to inquire about this pressing matter, your client will not be able to manage their finances and could face imminent bankruptcy. Therefore, calculating and keeping the end in mind is pivotal right from the start.

Can you imagine a writer writing a book without an end in their mind? Of course not. If they are not clear about the end, they can never write an engaging story. The same is the case when you either do your own business or advise your client about their business.

This is the significance of transferable value and the

transferable value dollar amount is super important. This book outlines the steps of The Clear Path to Cash blueprint strategy for helping you focus on funding your future. This first chapter will weave through the remaining steps as the basis for the financial decisions you will have to make. In later chapters, you will gain awareness on several key financial concepts that will give you or your client the opportunity to fund your dreams, bring clarity to your business vision, and establish a legacy in your respective industry. You'll do this while living a current lifestyle you can enjoy. You will be building a lifestyle-friendly business. One that funds your future while providing you with rewards today.

Chapter 3
THE HOME RUN FINANCIAL SYSTEM

No matter how orderly or precise a business owner maybe, nine times out of ten they will forget to concentrate on their financial statements. In most cases, these business owners are so caught up in the day-to-day running of the business that they completely overlook the most essential element. The reason why I am referring to financial statements as the most essential element is that without them, you will never have a basic understanding of your company's position. You NEED financial statements to not only be aware of your business's current estate but also predict its future progress. This is why, it is imperative for you, as a potential business owner, to pay close attention to your financial statements and plan your strategies and policies accordingly. You must not sporadically analyze these reports. On the contrary, you need to analyze these statements thoroughly and figure out the company's errors and mistakes. Even if you don't have the time to focus on these reports, you need to sacrifice your other endeavors and channel your energy towards financial statements.

Now, you must be thinking how do I achieve such a feat? Well, don't worry, you will be able to better understand the techniques from a situation I encountered some time ago. In 2011, when I was planning on buying a different business. I looked at all kinds of businesses from landscaping companies all the way to flower shops. I bet I looked at over 100 companies during that time. After the first few, I got frustrated because I was having trouble comparing these companies to each other.

As a result, I was quite perplexed, and I tried to analyze different aspects of those businesses. Yet still, I didn't arrive at an accurate conclusion. In the end, I wanted a way to compare company performance in a fast-simple way that incorporated all three of the financial statements. With the help of my learning and observation, I came up with a six steps matrix that I call a "Home Run Lineup". I referred to it as the Home Run Lineup because it touched all the bases. By bases, I mean every financial statement that can be used for business analysis. The good news is that this chapter is entirely dedicated to this home run lineup. This is a quick and simple way to analyze the financial health of any company, irrespective of the industry or size. At the same time, it is a seven-minute conversation with either yourself or your client to assess the business you or your client wants to analyze the performance of (not just for buying a company). By the end of this chapter, you will be able to:

- Identify the most critical measurement of profitability and health in a small business using all the financial statements.
- Learn how to have a quick, but meaningful conversation about the numbers using the Home Run Lineup Card.
- Gain trust and credibility with any business owner in one simple step.
- Set business owners up for success in making more money or getting a financing request.

The last two steps are specifically for advisors of small businesses and they can avail these steps to add layers to their success. However, before discussing the Home Run

Lineup, we first need to understand the purpose of all of the financial statements. Most of the people I have met, who don't have a finance background. As a result, they tend to lean on the income statement more heavily than the balance sheet and cash flow statement. Mainly, because it is simpler and much easier to understand. However, the other two statements expose a different side of the story and need to be considered when looking at a company's performance.

Income Statement

The income statement simply tells whether your business is viable. It is a report card for your business that tells if your business generates profit. While the income statement shows your business' profitability, it is good just for the period you're measuring. When that particular period ends, the income statement starts over.

Balance Sheet

The balance sheet represents the financial position of your business. In other words, it shows whether your company is in a good or a bad state. It states your assets, liabilities, and owner's equity. It is the culmination of every management decision because every decision is recorded on the balance sheet throughout the history of the company. Therefore, the balance sheet will illustrate the net worth or "book value" of your company.

Cash Flow Statement

The statement of cash flow shows where the cash in your business came from and went to. This report tells what exactly is going on in your business. In short, it is the tattletale of your business. It tells the story of how management sources and uses cash in their business. Hence, it is vital to understand the above three financial statements to reach a final decision.

The following are the six elements of the Home Run Lineup Worksheet. Analyzing these elements will not only help you to filter out the good from the bad businesses but it will also assist you in managing your or your client's existing business efficiently. Data for this analysis is taken from the three types of financial statements.

1. Trends
2. Expense Control
3. Debt to Equity Ratio
4. EBITDA/ Long Term Debt Availability
5. Mis-Financed Assets
6. Cash Flow Activity Pattern

Trends

Figure 3.1

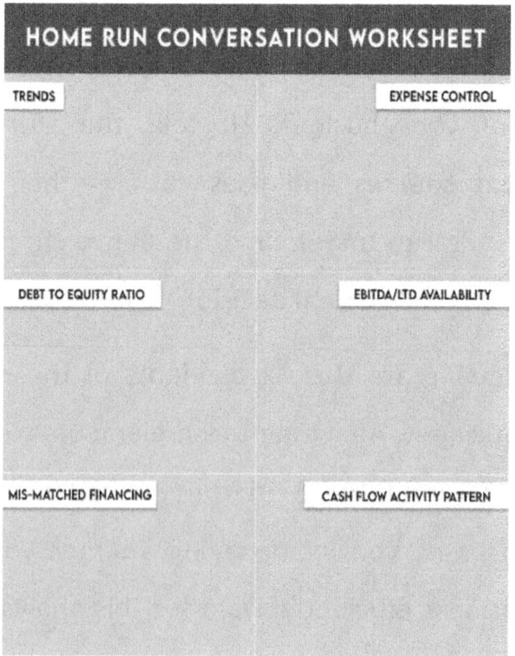

Trends are analyzed using the most popular financial statement i.e. Income Statement. In fact, it is something that we naturally do as part of looking at a company's financial position. When we look at trends, we are looking for the general direction they appear to be going and how the trends of specific items related to one another.

Trends are less impactful if we say things like the trend is up. That is only half the information we need to evaluate this portion of the Homerun Line-up. We have to also look at the magnitude of change to see if it's relevant. It is one thing for a trend to be up $100 over a year, and quite another for the trend to be up $1 million in the same time period. The magnitude of change matters.

Also notice, how I used dollars to describe the magnitude of change. Because we spend dollars and we can understand the value of anything easily if it is defined in terms of dollars. I often hear that "sales are up 10%". It indeed sounds good, but it forces me to convert 10% into dollars so I can understand it. You can't spend percentages. If you think you can tell me how many percent does a gallon of milk cost. Make sure you look at the changes in your accounts in terms of dollars.

Here are the four-line items I look at when analyzing trends.

SALES

1. Are they growing, declining or staying flat?
2. Ask why the trend seems to be moving this way.
3. Is it normal or is this a problem that needs to be addressed?
4. Stay focused on getting customers to buy – right product/service for the right price.

GROSS PROFIT

1. Which way is the gross profit trending?
2. 2. Is it moving in the same direction as sales?
3. Should it be or why are they different?
4. Ask about vendor pricing, relationships, efficiency, and pricing strategy.

OPERATING EXPENSE

1. Which direction is the operating expense trending?
2. What has the company increased and is it needed?

3. What are the current cuts or items that need justification for staying?
4. Compare operating expense categories to industry averages, like advertising.

NET PROFIT

1. Is this company making money or losing money?
2. What is the trend? Increasing or falling?
3. What are the prime contributors – gross profit, expenses, sales, or all?

Let's understand the trends with the example of a sample company. You can find a set of sample financial statements in the appendix of this book.

Figure 3.2

SAMPLE COMPANY TRENDS

		Year 1	Year 2	Year 3	Year 4	Year 5
↓ $1,190	Sales	$9,639	$8,925	$9,044	$8,092	$8,449
↓ $538	Gross Profit	$3,132	$2,892	$2,794	$2,549	$2,594
↓ $416	Operating Expenses	$2,844	$2,643	$2,560	$2,390	$2,428
↓ $101	Net Profit After Tax	$112	$48	$43	$2	$11

In the above income statement, you can see that the gross profit has declined by $538,000 over a period of five years. Generally, sales and gross profit move together in the same direction. If sales decline, gross profit also decreases. Similarly, if sales increase, then the gross profit also increases. In this example, we can say that sales and gross profit both are on a declining trend during the five years. What is interesting is the relationship. We expect these two accounts to move in the same direction is the company is managing to a consistent gross profit margin percentage. Sometimes you might see them move in opposite directions. This should get your attention. This means that something is happening that needs to be identified as either positive or negative.

Here are a couple of examples: If sales were down, but gross profit is up, we can celebrate. You would want to know why, but in general, this is a positive relationship. You are working (selling) less but making more money (increasing gross profit). The opposite relationship could indicate a problem if you were selling more and making less money. Chances are you have a higher cost of goods sold percentage like your vendors have increased your prices. You should investigate and take corrective action to recapture the gross profit dollars you had previously.

The second element is operating expenses. Operating expenses and gross profit/sales don't necessarily move together. Operating expenses completely depend upon the management's decision as to how and where they spend money. In this case, we see that operating expenses are trending down by $416,000. At first glance, this seems like a good thing. That means that management recognized the decrease in gross profit and started to cut expenses as a response.

When operating expenses are deducted from gross profit, the remaining amount is net profit. Net profit is just a result. There is nothing you can do directly to impact net profit; you have to work on one of the other three accounts we analyzed. The purpose for including it here is to show you the results of movement in sales, gross profit, and operating expenses. The sample company is down $101,000. This is a significant amount and should cause you to look for the cause. In this case, it is pretty obvious that a decrease in sales created the problem.

After identifying these patterns, we will move on to the next step i.e. Expense Control.

Expense Control

As I mentioned above that operating expenses and gross profit don't necessarily move together because they depend upon the management's decision. They don't go up or down with respect to change in any element. However, there is a hard and fast rule to control expenses. The rule is, *"Change in operating expenses should mirror the change in gross profit."*

Gross profit is the money you have available to spend, whereas operating expenses show how you spend that money. As a business manager or advisor, your goal is to make sure to keep your operating expenses flat even when the gross profit increases. This way your business can make more money. Now let's connect to the above sample company's income statement again. In the above example, operating expenses have declined by $416,000 over a period of five years, which is less than the decline in gross profit of $538,000. It shows that even after a decline in gross profit, the management did not control its expenses accordingly. The operating expenses should have been cut down another $100,000 to maintain the net profit of the company.

The reduction in operating expenses compared to the reduction in gross profit should always be equal or greater. When this difference shrinks, the management should take action to control it. Many companies start laying off their employees to cut down operating expenses. If the management doesn't take timely action, it can even lead to the dissolution of the business. Simply put, when you have less money to spend (less gross profit), you should spend less money (fewer operating expenses).

The following chart can be used to evaluate the difference in gross profit and operating expenses movement.

Figure 3.3

EXPENSE CONTROL

	GROSS PROFIT	Use this chart to evaluate differences in movements	OPERATING EXPENSES
INCREASE IN AMOUNT	⬆ ☺	If GP is ____ OE: = ✓ > ✓ < X	⬆ ⚠
DECREASE IN AMOUNT	⬇ ⚠	If GP is ____ OE: = ✓ > X < ✓	⬇ ☺

Debt to Equity Ratio

The Debt to Equity ratio compares the amount of money you borrowed for your business with the amount of money you invested in it yourself. It shows how much you believe in your company. Businesses choose debt financing because it is the best way to pay less taxes. After all, the interest you pay for the money you borrowed becomes an expense that lowers net profit. However, a higher debt to equity ratio of a company represents a higher risk for shareholders because it signifies that the company has been aggressive in financing its growth with debt. This ratio is an interesting one for small business owners because it causes them to choose a side between the banker and the accountant. Naturally, business owners look to these two as trusted advisors for their company, but when it comes to this ratio, they give the business owner opposite advice on what to do.

To understand why they would differ, you have to understand the objectives of both the banker and the accountant. First, the banker wants to give you money. One of the ways banks earn revenue is by giving loans to its customers and earning interest on that loan. So, the banker wants you to have a strong cash flow and a lower amount of outstanding debt. The accountant, on the other hand, wants you to pay the least amount of taxes possible each year. We pay taxes on net profit and net profit is then transferred onto the balance sheet in the form of retained earnings. In other words, owners' equity. Therefore, when we reduce our net profit with higher expenses, we are also reducing the amount of equity being captured by the company's operations.

Debt to Equity ratio is calculated by dividing Total Liabilities with Total Equity. 2.5 is a good target ratio to achieve. A 2.5 means that for every $1 an owner has invested in their company; they have let the bank invest an additional $2.50. Lower than 3 is GOOD and shows less risk. Higher than 3 indicates more risk to bankers or investors. The data to calculate this ratio is extracted from the company's balance sheet.

Think about it this way. When you buy a house, you typically put down 20% of the purchase price, and the bank loans you the remaining 80%. 80% is the liability and 20% is your equity. Divide these two numbers and you arrive at a Debt to Equity Ratio of 4.0. This means for every $1 you put into the house, you let the bank put in $4 and everyone is happy. To show a higher risk to the bank, take the same example, and only put in 10% of the purchase price. Divide 90% of the price, by the 10% you put down and the result is a Debt to Equity Ratio of 9.0. The bank has more risk when the number is higher.

Consider the following sample balance sheet.

Figure 3.4

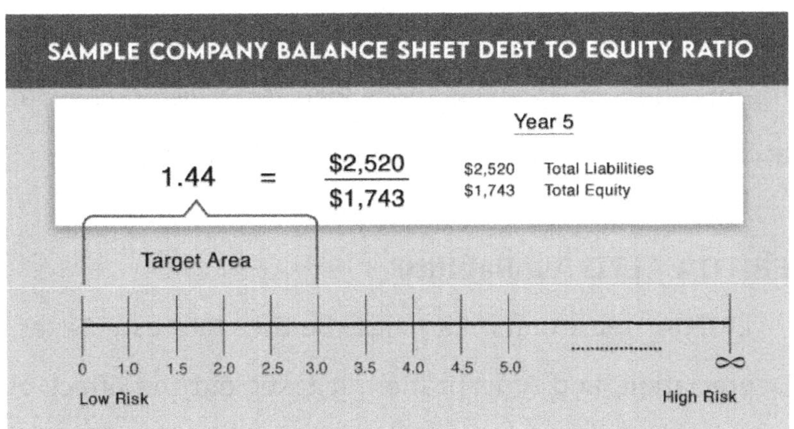

In the following balance sheet, the debt to equity ratio is 1.44, which is less than 2.5. It is a good ratio, and lenders and investors can trust this company while making business decisions.

So, who do you listen to as a business owner, the banker, or the accountant? Well, it depends on the answer to this question. "Do I think I will need a loan next year to fund my company's growth or operation?" Notice I said NEXT YEAR. That's because if you need to apply for a loan, the banker will be looking at how the Debt to Equity Ratio trends in your company. They want to know that you have skin in the game through your investment in retained earnings. If you think you might need a loan next year, start managing your debt to equity ratio today. On the other hand, if you have no intention of applying for a loan, then listen to your accountant and pay as little tax as you legally can.

EBITDA / LTD Availability

EBITDA represents Earnings Before Interest, Taxes, Depreciation, and Amortization. It takes out the effect of accounting and financing decisions. Or you can say it is a proxy word for cash flow. It is the measure of the company's overall financial performance. Use the following chart to calculate your company's EBITDA.

Figure 3.5

SAMPLE COMPANY EBITDA

Earnings (Net Profit After Tax)	$11,000		
BEFORE	+		
Interest	$154,000		EBITDA
Taxes	$2,000	=	$385,000
Depreciation	$218,000		
Amortization	$0		

According to the Sample Company Income Statement in the Appendix, EBITDA of the sample business is $11000 + $154,000 + $2,000 + $218,000 + $0 = $385,000.

While working with banks around the country, I was able to determine that although every bank has a different calculation, they all arrive at an amount that is approximately 3 times EBITDA for a company's long term borrowing capacity. So, if we multiply the sample company's EBITDA by 3, we get an approximate Long-Term

Debt Capacity (LTD Capacity) that this company might be able to afford with their cash flow. LTD shows the approximate amount of long-term debt your business might qualify for. As a business owner or advisor, you must know that how much amount you can borrow from a bank. Based on this information, you can adjust your financing decisions. For example, according to figure 5, the sample company is qualified to borrow up to $1,155,000 in long-term debt. However, this is the total amount. If you have already borrowed any funds, then that amount should be deducted from your LTD capacity. Refer to Sample Company's Balance Sheet in the Appendix, using Year 5 to determine if they have any LTD on the books. The sample company has already borrowed long-term funds of $713,000. So, the amount they might apply for is $442,000 ($1,155,000 - $713,000).

Figure 3.6

SAMPLE COMPANY LONG TERM DEBT AVAILABILITY

EBITDA				Long Term Debt Capacity
$385,000	x 3		=	$1,155,000

LTD Capacity		LTD on Balance Sheet		Long Term Debt Capacity Available
$1,155,000	-	$713,000	=	$442,000

Mis-Financing

The fifth element of the Home Run Lineup Worksheet is Mis-Financing. This is the silent killer of your business. And the funny part is most of us don't even think about it. However, no one ever mis-finances their company on purpose. It generally occurs during everyday routine transactions. It happens when you use the wrong loan products for the assets you buy. For example, you use your credit card to buy a house. You wouldn't do that right? I mean, you could get a ton of airline miles out of the deal, but it would cost you a fortune. The house you buy is a long-term asset, whereas the type of loan you are using to buy it is short-term i.e. credit card. Generally, the rate of interest on the credit card is about 15 to 20%. However, if you use the long-term mortgage to buy the same house, you will pay about 4 to 5% rate of interest. A huge difference, isn't it? This is because short-term money is more expensive than the long-term. If you use the wrong loan product to finance your assets, it will eventually rob your company of cash in the form of paying higher interest.

The best way to start checking for mis-financing is by looking at the balance sheet. Check the business' gross fixed assets (GFA), long-term debt (LTD), and retained earnings (RE). The change in GFA between periods must be equal to a corresponding change in LTD and/or RE. This is a simple variation of the Basic Accounting Formula: Assets = Liabilities + Equity. By narrowing it down to only GFA, LTD, and RE, we are focusing in on assets you bought and the method you used to pay for them. In this case, we want you to buy GFA with cash, long term debt, or a combination of both. An increase in GFA means that you bought something. There should be an equal increase in LTD if you used a term loan to finance the purchase. There may be an increase in

RE if you used cash to pay for the purchase. Remember that cash in your company can be derived from profit from your operation. At the end of the period, an increase in profit means that RE was increased with a corresponding increase in cash, (or Accounts Receivable to be collected as cash).

By leaving out Current Liabilities from this equation, we can surmise that if the mis-financing equation does not equal, the purchase was probably made with a short term credit product like a credit card or a line of credit. If your company's mis-financing calculation does not equal; call your banker for help. It may put more cash in your pocket by lowering your interest expense.

The effects of improper debt structure can be debilitating to a business. Finding mis-financing in its early stages can help to mitigate the effects it has on a business. The rule here is that the length of your loan must match the useful life of your asset. That is, if you can depreciate an asset for 5 years, you should use a 5-year term loan to finance it. The following chart can help you while analyzing your business.

Figure 3.7

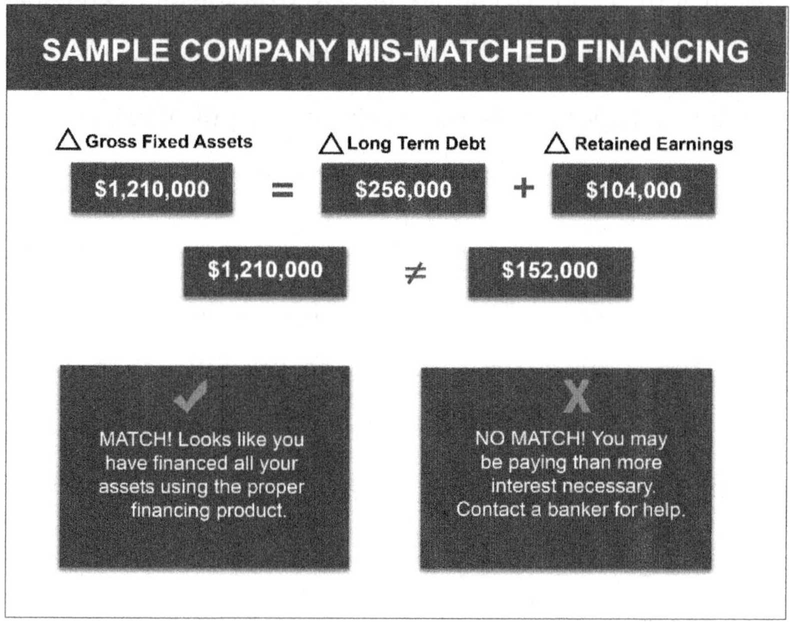

Cash Flow Activity Pattern

I call this element the Tattle Tale of a business. It tells the reader exactly where the cash came in from and how you used it. Your business is alive. It is a dynamic and fluid machine capable of way more than we often give it credit for. Just like the human body, your company can generate a lot of positive energy and accomplish things that most people can only imagine. Cash is called the lifeblood of a company because it is one of the business's most essential needs. Your company requires a steady supply of money to function properly. Cash flow is the prime contributing factor for the survival of any business, no matter how awesome of product or service you might have.

This goes beyond just showing a net profit at the end of the month. If your company's ability to generate and use cash is inefficient, you can go bankrupt pretty fast. Matter of fact, over 50,000 businesses fail every quarter, and 7 out of the top 10 reasons for failure involved some level of poor cash flow management. It has also been noted that out of approximately 50,000 businesses that file bankruptcy each year had a net profit on their income statement.

How does a company make a profit and go out of business? They ended up earning a net profit on paper, but the cash never materialized in the bank. This element takes into account cash flow from operating, financing, and investing activities. The following chart can be used to identify how your company is performing based on your cash inflows and outflows. More importantly, it tells you how the management of any company generates and uses cash in their business.

Figure 3.8

SAMPLE COMPANY CASH FLOW ACTIVITY PATTERN

Cash Flow Statement Summary	Year 5	
Beginning Cash	$39,000	
Operating Activities	($102,000)	Operating Activities: −
Investing Activities	$182,000	Investing Activities: +
Financing Activities	($18,000)	Financing Activities: −
Ending cash	$101,000	

The figure above is the sample summarized cash flow statement. According to the rules mentioned above, in the symbolic form, it is - + -. It depicts a struggling business where the company management is trying to cover its operating shortfalls and long-term debt payments by selling its assets. This is a recipe for disaster. The only reason to buy assets is to generate revenue and profit. So, when a company is selling its assets to cover expenses, they are also reducing their ability to generate revenue and profit. This is an indicator that the company is in a death spiral.

Below is a legend of all 8 symbol combinations that can appear on a company's cash flow statement summary.

Figure 3.9

CASH FLOW ACTIVITY PATTERN LEGEND

	OPERATING ACTIVITIES	INVESTING ACTIVITIES	FINANCING ACTIVITIES	INTERPRETATION
1	+	+	+	This company is building cash and is highly liquid.
2	+	−	−	This company generates cash from operations and is buying assets and paying debt and owners.
3	+	+	−	This company is using cash from operations and selling assets to pay debt and /or owners.
4	+	−	+	This company uses cash from operations and from borrowing /investment to expand.
5	−	+	+	This company covers cash flow problems by selling assets and by borrowing /investment.
6	−	−	+	This company is growing but has shortages from operations and buying assets with debt.
7	−	+	−	This company is trying to stay in business by selling their assets to cover expenses.
8	−	−	−	This company is burning through cash reserves to cover shortfalls and pay creditors/investors..

As a business owner or financial advisor, it is pivotal that you can analyze a business. Your efficient analysis can save you from huge losses. This doesn't mean that you can't make any mistakes. However, the gist of this chapter is to put your maximum efforts before making any crucial decisions.

This is another reason I created the Homerun Line Up. In just 7 minutes per month, I could get a complete picture of what my company's financial position. If any of these elements were bad, I knew where to look to find the problem. If they looked good to me, I'd just go back to my business routine of trying to provide the best service possible for my clients.

Here is what the completed Homerun Line Up would look like for our sample company. As you can see, there are plenty of problems for the management team to address.

Figure 3.10

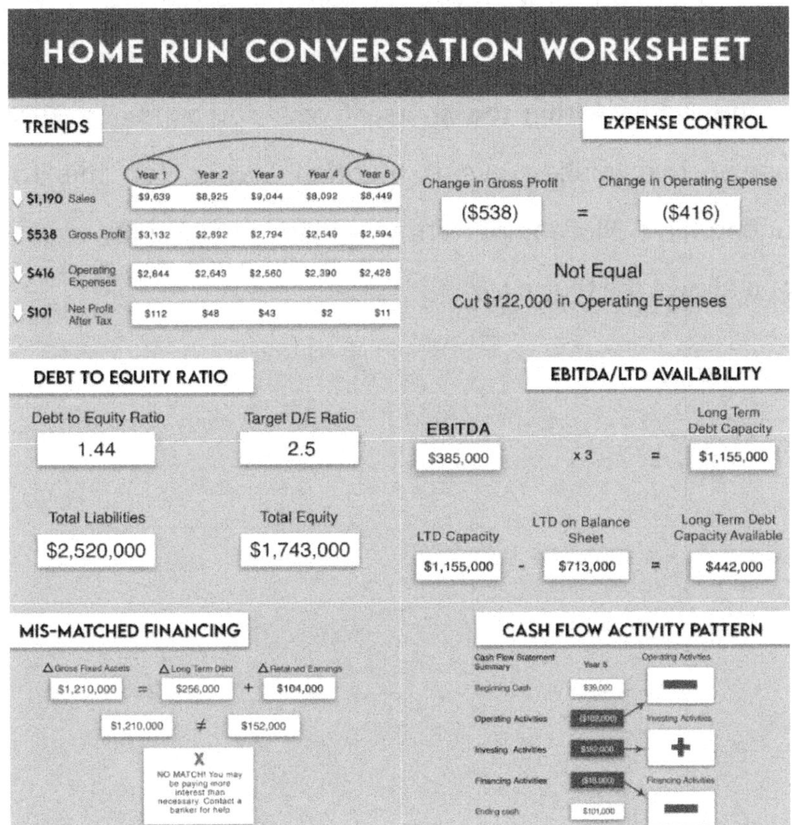

One of the best pieces of advice I ever received in my life is "Control what you can control". Simple, but elegant. These five words resonated with me. They gave me clarity for everything that came next in my professional and personal lives. These words cut through the fog of chaos and provided guidance. So, as a way of paying it forward, I say to you, control what you can control. Look at the entire situation and spend your creative and critical thinking skills on operating within the limits of your surroundings. This perspective makes every situation easier for me to understand. More importantly, it helps mitigate my stress and allows me to grow.

Chapter 4
FIND HIDDEN CASH WITH THIS METHOD

Whenever you feel unwell and sick, you visit a doctor, right?

How do you describe your condition to the doctor?

You will most probably tell them about the signs and symptoms you have been experiencing. Based on this description, the doctor will try to identify the possible causes of your sickness. Quite simple, isn't it?

Our businesses work the same way. They also have some signs and symptoms which you need to analyze from time to time to make sure that your business is healthy. I know you might be wondering what these signs and symptoms are. In the next four chapters, you will get to learn a technique to identify many of the signs and symptoms that will help you understand whether or not your business is healthy. Whenever you visit a doctor, you have to go through several steps before you can conclude your health.

Normally, the doctor will ask you for your medical history along with any other information about your present symptoms. When they have sufficient data, they will move toward the next step and will conduct a physical examination.

This physical examination will give the doctor somewhat of an idea regarding your health. However, this is still not enough to reach a proper conclusion. After collecting all the information about your health, the doctor will conduct a series of tests to guide his diagnosis of the problem. They try to decipher the root cause behind your condition and officially move to the next step. The next step is also very important as it gives the doctor solid proof that you are suffering from a specific ailment. In this step, the doctor orders the required tests to review the results of the tests, and then finally acts on them.

After extensively reviewing the results of the tests, the doctor will eventually reach a final diagnosis. They can either make this decision on their own or through the help of their peers. Following this, they will give you a consultation. This consultation will not only describe your medical condition, but the doctor will also prescribe you medicine to treat the ailment effectively. Without following these steps, the doctor, no matter how efficient they may be, cannot perform their duty. And, even if they did, they are bound to make the wrong judgment and could even damage their patient. To avoid this situation, the doctor needs to follow protocols and shouldn't try to overlook any procedure whatsoever.

If you were to view this scenario from a business perspective, you will come to know that 7/10 entrepreneurs fail at maintaining their businesses. While there could be many reasons behind their failure, the most common cause is none other than mismanaged cash flow. Cash flow allows your business to survive in any concerned industry. Your business is a dynamic and fluid machine capable of way more than we often give it credit for. Just like the human body, your company can generate a lot of positive energy and accomplish things that most people can only imagine. The similarity to the body doesn't stop there. Your company also has a huge basic need that it requires to survive.

Cash is called the lifeblood of a company because it is one of the business's most essential needs. Your company requires a steady supply of money to function properly. Cash flow is the prime contributing factor for the survival of any business, no matter how awesome your product or service maybe. This goes beyond just showing a net profit at the end of the month. If your company's ability to generate and use cash is inefficient, you can go bankrupt pretty fast. Over 50,000 businesses fail every quarter, and it is estimated that at least 35% of the failed owners believed their company was making money based on their financial statements. They could see a net profit every month, but the cash never materialized in the bank.

As a small business owner, I always got excited to see a month with a profitable income statement. That meant that customers were buying, and I was being smart with how I spent money. At least on paper. There were those times where I could see that I made money, but it just didn't make it into the bank account. I still felt like I was struggling to pay bills, even though the financial statements told me I shouldn't have a problem. Where was the cash going?

This is where the difference between profit and cash sets in. I had to realize that the income statement was limited to recording my business process but didn't account for actual dollars hitting the bank account. So, I went on a treasure hunt for dollars within my own company. Here is what I found.

There were five silent killers of cash flow, where cash was hidden from the income statement. These five areas were killing my cash flow and making it harder to stay in business. Once I made the connection between cash flow and profit, I was able to change the whole trajectory of my business and its future. If you feel this way, look here.

1. **Accounts receivable** – Make sure you are being paid as quickly as possible. I had a service-based business, where my largest expense was payroll. I had to educate my customers to treat my invoices more like a payroll expense and pay more frequently.
2. **Accounts payable** – This may sound a little odd, but don't pay much earlier than the due date, unless you are getting a discount. This is like a free loan and retains cash in your company.

3. **Inventory management** – Learn to set your base level inventory amounts. This is where you have just enough of an item between orders. Look at history and match your orders to your customers. If they normally buy 10 of a particular item in a week, then you should have 10-12 on hand. Your quantity on hand should match your base level (or par) at the beginning of an order cycle.

4. **Expense control** – There is a hard and fast rule here. The change in operating expenses should mirror the change in gross profit. If gross profit is reduced by $10k, then you should also reduce your operating expense by $10k. Simply put, when you have less money, you should spend less money.

5. **Mis-financing** – Almost none of us check for this regularly, but we should. This is where you have purchased a long-term asset, with a short-term product. Like buying a house with a credit card. You wouldn't do this unless you wanted the miles! No, you wouldn't do this because the cost of borrowing is too high, and it would increase your interest expense. The length of the loan should match the life of the asset is the rule.

In most cases, I have found that entrepreneurs do not know to manage the inflow and outflow of funds within their company. And, because of this, they are unable to meet their financial obligations nor earn decent revenues. To rectify this situation, you need fully analyze your company using ratio analysis to scope out certain lucrative opportunities. Ratio analysis will help you understand your business's operational inefficiencies and improve them considerably. Additionally, you need to be aware of the techniques of spotting hidden cash opportunities. Ideally, you should not let your lack of knowledge force you to incur unnecessary expenses and impair your profitability altogether. In my personal experience, you or any other entrepreneur can check the current condition of your company through four simple steps. In other words, you need to become a financial doctor and figure out the true picture of your company. Much like a medical doctor, you need to go through 4 stages in order to predict the financial health of your organization. These four stages include:

1. **Test** – gather your financial information and look for the financial indicators that a problem may exist. Think of

this as a fact-finding mission to find out the history and current symptoms of the "patient" – your company.

2. **Analyze** – compare the results of your tests to what you expect. Your results are the symptoms that lead to diagnosing the actual cause. In this phase, we are looking to answer the question: Where does it "hurt"?

3. **Diagnose** – after analyzing the financial statements, ratios will help you find the cause of any financial problems your company may have. The "effect" that stands out during the analysis phase points directly at the area of your business "causing" the pain.

4. **Treat** – the diagnosis will point you to specific areas needing treatment. It is time to prescribe the patient with a treatment plan. Simply put, you will turn the results of the ratio analysis into action that have the greatest positive impact on your company's health.

As a capable financial doctor, you need to treat your business using this methodology and try to weed out hidden cash opportunities. However, before you conduct this analysis, you need to make sure you have a full set of financial statements. For the sample company in this book, I have 5 years' worth of income statement, balance sheet, and cash flow statement data. You don't need to have 5 years' worth, but 3 to 5 years is a good target. Banks typically ask you for 3 years' worth of financial statements if you apply for a loan, so you might already have this available. All of these documents are essential to The Financial Doctor methodology.

In the sample company statements, the first year will be the oldest year of the company while the fifth year will be the newest year of performance. You can use my sample company documents to follow along with the walkthrough of The Financial Doctor Method. Once you have these documents in place, you will also need to acquire the key ratio industry averages for your company. These industry averages can be obtained from the bank or online. Another way to compare your performance is to outline your current business goals in the place of industry averages for each ratio. The industry averages or your business goals will allow you to compare your company's performance with other players in the market and identify where you have challenges and opportunities.

Then, finally, you will need the ratio analysis worksheet and the hidden cash worksheet. Through the ratio analysis worksheet, you can calculate a variety of ratios and use them to make a reasonable judgment. The Hidden Cash Worksheet helps you calculate the financial impact of not meeting your desired outcomes and helps you set a priority for making meaningful changes in your company. Once you have these documents, you can finally commence the financial doctor analysis and streamline your business. In the next 4 chapters, we will cover each step of the Financial Doctor Method and unravel all hidden cash opportunities.

Chapter 5
TEST

The Financial Doctor Method

After you have gathered the necessary documents and items needed for the Financial Doctor methodology, you are finally in a position to move towards the first step. The first step of the Financial Doctor deals directly with the most commonly used 14 ratios in the business world. To truly test a company's financial health, there can be no better alternative than ratio analysis.

Ugh, I'm already bored. Don't get me wrong. I'm a numbers nerd deep down in my core, but I hate reading about how to calculate ratios. What I didn't realize was that I would hate writing about them even more. This is my third attempt to write this chapter and after a sleepless night; I decided to scrap my original plan to teach you how to do the math.

I mean, let's face it. There are plenty of computer programs out there to do the math for you. What I needed as a business owner what to understand what the numbers meant so I could make more money, get a bank loan, or grow my business. So, I decided to give you some real talk about what these ratios mean to you in a way that most people can understand.

In this step, we will use the ratio analysis worksheet to TEST the data in our sample financial statements. Just don't expect me to drag you through this the same old boring dribble you can already find on the internet. Instead, I've added **REAL TALK** to help you apply to your life.

Ratio Analysis Worksheet

The above worksheet gives us an overview of the 14 ratios used by the business world and what category each ratio belongs to. You can use the sample company's financial statements or even your own company's numbers to practice calculating these ratios. If you prefer to let a computer do the math, just download and use the Ratio Analysis Spreadsheet from my website: www.cashflowmike.com.

To sum it up, ratios can be classified into four distinct categories. These four categories include:

1. **Liquidity** – the speed that you can convert your assets to cash to pay your short-term bills.
2. **Solvency** – the company's ability to pay its long term debts.
3. **Profitability** – your ability to use your resources to generate more revenue than you spend.
4. **Asset Management** – how well do you use your assets to create additional cash flow and revenue for your business.

Liquidity

Out of these four categories, the first category deals with how fast you can convert your assets into cash. More often than not, people get confused with the term 'liquidity' and do not know how to calculate these ratios. In order to avoid this confusion, you must understand that liquidity means the cash you can spend. To conduct this analysis, you will need to calculate two distinct ratios. These ratios include the current and quick ratios. These ratios tell you how fast your business is generating cash and whether or not you can support yourself in the long haul.

REAL TALK: Can You Generate Enough Cash To Pay for Your Own Operation This Year?

Current Ratio

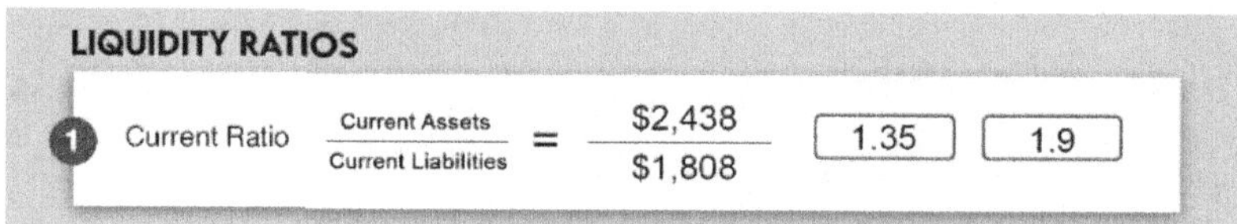

The current ratio measures how fast you can convert your assets into cash within one year. In other words, this ratio also determines how much money you have to pay all your liabilities within a year.

To read it, just compare how your ratio measures up against the industry average. The higher this number is the better. It means that you have access to more cash than you owe on a short-term basis. At a minimum, a good current ratio would be a 2.0. That means you have $2 in your checking account for every $1 you owe on a credit card. In our sample company, the result is 1.35. At least they can cover their own obligations, but as you can see when we compare it to the industry target of 1.9. It is considerably lower.

REAL TALK: Can I Still Pay for My Day-To-Day Operation, If I Need Money In 90 Days?

Quick Ratio

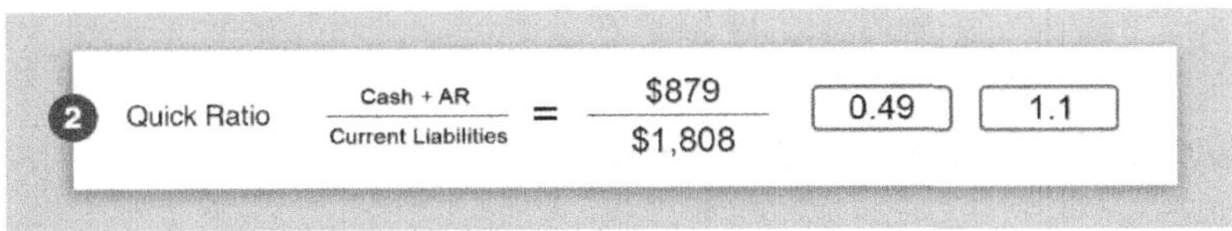

On the other hand, the quick ratio is a little different from the current ratio. This is because a quick ratio depicts the assets which can be converted within 90 days - when calculating this ratio you need to leave out the inventory and prepaid expenses. The reason why you leave out inventory is that you probably can't sell all your inventory in 90 days unless you discount it substantially. Also, prepaid expenses need to be removed, since as once you have already paid for these expenses, chances are that you won't receive them back anytime soon. It is a stingy ratio which deals with assets that can be converted far quicker than the current ratio. But, it can tell you something about the inventory you have on the shelf. If the result is significantly lower than your current ratio, chances are your company is heavily dependent on inventory. In an ideal scenario, your ratio needs to be at least 1.0 or close to 1.0. The reason is that a company is expected to be able to pay for its day to day operation. In a well-run company, your current assets MUST be able to pay for your current liabilities. All the while, the sale of fixed assets needs to cover any long-term debts or liabilities incurred by the company.

As a final note, the quick ratio is often called the “acid test”. The acid test was a quick method used by gold prospectors to find “real gold” by using nitric acid on metals brought in to be traded. Gold was resistant to dissolving and therefore easy to distinguish from “fool’s gold”. Using this line of thought, you can think of the quick ratio as a way to find the gold in your company. Our sample company looks to be in trouble here. Their quick ratio is only 0.49. This means they can’t cover their current obligations. What makes it worse is that the rest of the industry can. The industry average is 1.1.

Solvency

Putting aside liquidity, you must also test your company based on its solvency. Solvency deals with your ability to pay your long-term debt obligations. Additionally, it tells others how much you believe in your company and what you are willing to invest in your own brand. Let's face it, investors and bankers want to see that you have "skin in the game" before they are willing to take a chance on your company. The ratio that shows them you care and can efficiently use debt within your company is to calculate the debt to equity ratio.

REAL TALK: How Much Have I Let the Bank Put into My Company Compared to How Much I Put In?

Debt to Equity Ratio

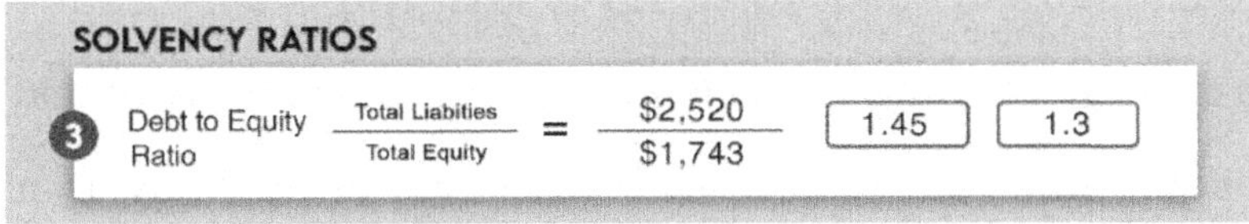

In this ratio, you must be aware that your banker and accountant will give you the opposite advice. This is mainly because the banker and accountant have opposite goals.

The accountant wants to limit your tax exposure by reducing your net profit through increased expenses. This is because companies are taxed on net profit. The increased expenses will lower your net profit, but it also decreases your expected equity. This is due to the fact that net profit gets moved onto the balance sheet in the form of retained earnings at the end of a month, quarter, or year.

The banker, however, wants you to have a higher amount of equity on your balance sheet. The amount they can lend is directly related to your own “skin in the game”. A lower equity amount could indicate that you, yourself, do not trust in your company’s future and might make securing someone else's investment a lot more difficult.

Now, what should the debt to equity ratio be? Your debt to equity ratio needs to be 2.5 or less. This is because the bank is more comfortable lending $2.50 for every dollar you put into the company yourself. It’s important to know that you want this number to be 2.5 or less on a trending basis. A higher number shows that your creditors have more at risk than you do. The higher the number, the more dependent on debt your company is to operate. So, if, you think you might need a loan to grow in the future, manage your debt to equity ratio to below 2.5. Here's a hint, you might have to pay a little more tax to get there.

On the other hand, if you won't need any funding in the next year to grow, then by all means listen to your accountant and pay less tax.

The sample company is actually doing ok in this area. They have a debt to equity ratio of 1.45, which is in line with the industry average of 1.3.

Profitability

If you want to know how well a company uses its resources to operate, look no further than its profitability ratios. They will tell you if they can generate more revenue than they spend, using all of the resources at their disposal. These are the most commonly understood business ratios in the test phase of The Financial Doctor Method.

REAL TALK: How Much Do I Have Left Over from A Sale? Gross Profit Margin

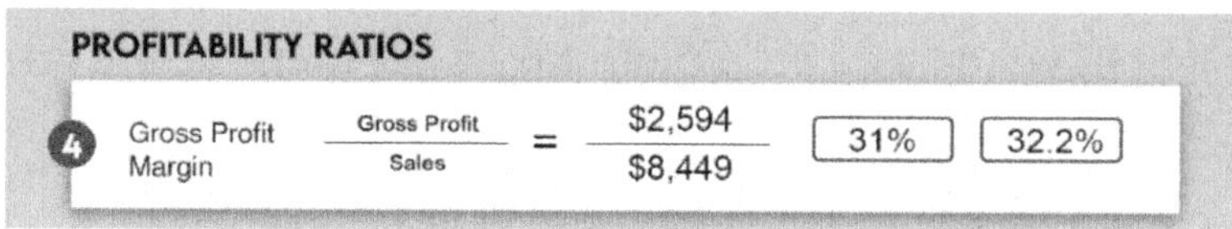

In my experience, the gross profit is the most important number on the income statement. The reason why I say this is because this is the only place, we can get cash and spend it openly. You can't spend sales, only the remaining value after your direct expenses are paid.

Successful business owners know that they must manage their business to a constant gross profit margin percentage. It is the pillar of your pricing strategy and help you determine if you can pay your monthly expenses.

However, to judge whether this number is good or bad, you must compare it with the industry average. One of the issues with using the industry average is making sure that you are categorizing your direct expenses, or your cost of goods sold similar to others in the same industry. If there is a large difference between your company's performance and the industry, you might not be classifying expenses in the same manner as your peers. If you are comparing apples with oranges, you are bound to see a huge difference. However, if you are comparing the same item, the difference may be small or even negligible. A large difference might mean you are including extra items in your cost of goods as compared to your competitors. This could also have a profound impact on your gross profit margin. As a result, you need to make sure you are making the right comparison.

Don't forget that cash flow doesn't happen without maximizing this number or getting as much from every sale as your customers will allow. Without a healthy gross profit margin, your company funds will dry up quickly.

Again, the sample company is close to the industry average, so no real cause for concern here. However, because it is a little lower, there might be an opportunity to find hidden cash here. More on that in a later chapter.

REAL TALK: How Much Do I Have Left Over at The End of The Month, Quarter, or Year?

Net Profit Margin

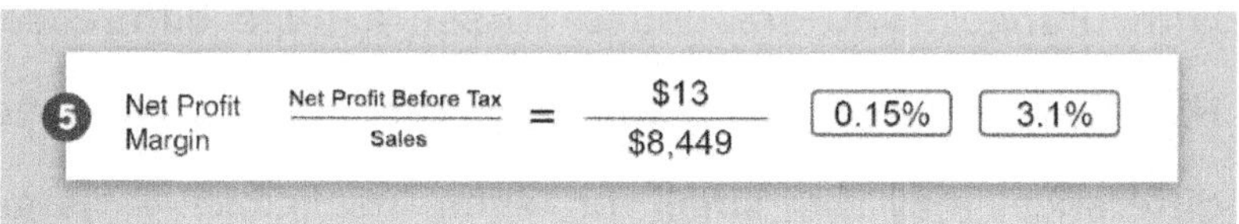

Other than the gross profit margin, you should also focus on the net profit margin. In a nutshell, the net profit margin is nothing but the result of your operations. Since it is the result of your operations, you cannot fix this value on its own. On the contrary, you need to fix your gross profit, sales, and operating expenses to make a change in the net profit margin. Let's say, in our sample company case, the net profit before tax is $13,000, and the total sales amount to $8,449,000.

Once you divide these two values, you will come at a result of 0.15%. This net profit margin represents that your company is not making any money and is probably near or at the breakeven point. Even though this margin is really low, you still need to compare it with industry margins in order to get a clear idea of your brand's position.

REAL TALK: How Much of Every Dollar I Invest in Equipment Comes Back to Me In The Form of Profit?

Return on Assets

This ratio tells us how much profit you are receiving from the money you invested in assets or equipment. You must know that the only reason to purchase an asset is to earn revenue and/or profit from it. In other words, the return on asset shows you how much of every dollar you invested becomes profit. To calculate the return on assets, you can take $13,000 as net profit before tax and $4.3 million as total assets. When you divide these two values, you will come to a result of 0.003%. This means that you are only making a third of a penny from your assets. This is a highly detrimental position for a company, and it tells you that you are underutilizing your assets. In order to increase this ratio, you need to ensure that all your equipment and assets are being used regularly by your staff and workforce. Any asset which is not in use needs to be discarded, sold, or removed from the balance sheet. This single measure will dramatically improve your Return on Assets and allow you to focus on other areas of your operations.

REAL TALK: Should I Have Invested in Something Other Than This Business?

Return on Investments (ROI)

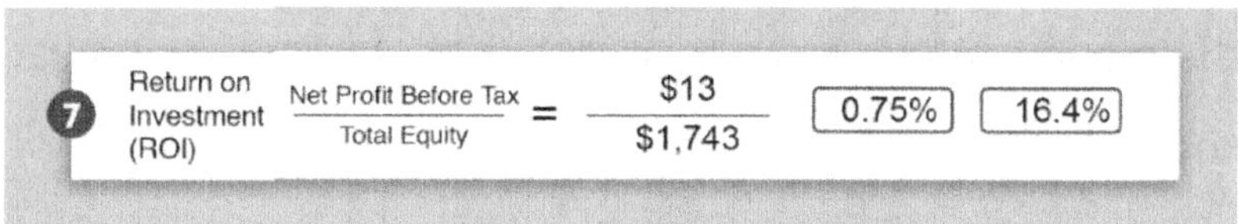

Upon discovering your company's return on assets, you need to turn your attention towards the last type of profitability ratio, Return on Investment. I am pretty sure you have heard the term Return on Investment throughout your business journey. Most entrepreneurs are fixated on this ratio and want to calculate it as soon as possible. You need to understand that Return on Investment is primarily used to compare several investment opportunities. As an entrepreneur, you have the choice of investing in multiple financial instruments such as the stock market, treasury bills, bonds, and deposit interest. And, through Return on Investment, you can find out which investment is more beneficial to you personally. Although you can use return on investment for different purposes, it is used predominantly to avail the best investment opportunity in the market. In order to understand Return on Investment, we can look at the sample company's financial statements. Net profit before tax is $13,000 and total equity is $1,743. If we were to divide both these values, we get a result of 0.75 or 75 basis points. This Return on Investment is less than 1.0% and it clearly represents that your company is not earning anything from their investment.

As a matter of fact, if the company was 30 or 40 years old, the change in the value of the original currency used to buy this company might have secured a far better return on investment than your present result if we put the money in a coffee can in the back yard. To make sure this is a good investment, compare your ROI with the industry average so that you will know you that you made the right decision.

In our case, let's take the industry average to be 16.4%. This industry average represents that your competitors are getting a higher rate of return than you are in the sample company. So, you have to ask yourself if investing your hard-earned money in a business that makes considerably less than average is worth it. Or you could look at an under-performing ROI for a company as an opportunity to make more money with the current level of investment. Meaning, with better management, this company should make more money. Aside from this, the ROI can also be used to help you calculate the potential market value of your company. You see, some valuation calculations use a “multiple” of another number like revenue or EBITDA.

The multiple is determined by taking either the current or expected ROI for an investment in your company. You simply divide 100 by the percentage rate of return you want. For example, 100/10% = 10X or ten times as a multiple. In a later chapter, called The Simple Valuation Formula, I’ll give you an easy way to put a value on your company using ROI to calculate a fair multiple for a company.

Asset management

Once you’ve confirmed or denied the fact that you are using your company’s assets to generate more revenue than you spend, it's time to calculate the speed that cash moves through your company. I call this the Speed of Cash. This category mainly deals with the cash conversion cycle. And, through these ratios, you can tell how well you bring the money in, how effectively you use it, how fast do we collect it, and how quickly do we pay it. These are the primary elements of asset management and the working capital cycle of your company. Your goal here is to go FAST! Stale money will not do your company any good.

REAL TALK: How Much in Sales Will A One Dollar Investment in A Piece of Equipment Generate?

Sales to Assets

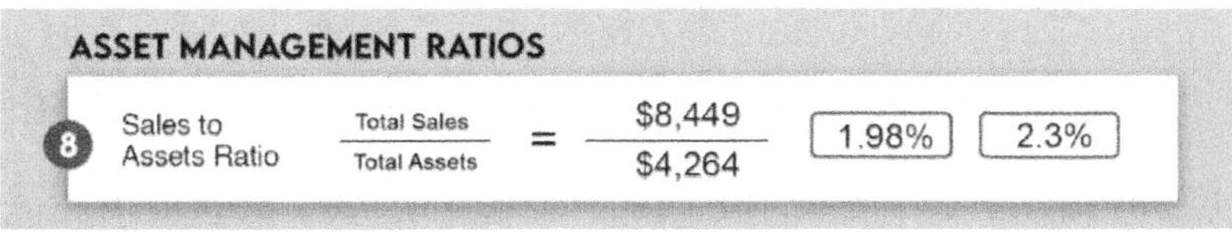

Among these ratios, the first ratio, Sales to Assets, estimates the total revenue or profit you earn from your equipment. In other words, through this ratio, you can determine how many dollars in sales are generated by investing one dollar in a piece of equipment or asset. So, to calculate this ratio, you have to divide your sales number by total assets. This ratio is a turnover ratio you can use to help forecast how many additional sales can be earned from a newly purchased piece of equipment in a company. You can also use it to compare how effectively you are using your assets compared to others in your industry. Here is an example of how to calculate the difference between you and your competitor.

To calculate this ratio, we can take our sample company's sales of $8.4 million and total assets of $4.3 million. Dividing these two values, we get the result of 1.98. This means that for every dollar you invest in equipment, you are generating $1.98 in sales.

After finding out this ratio, you need to compare it with the industry average. In our situation, let's suppose the industry average is 2.3. This implies that your competitors are earning $2.30 in sales from every dollar they invested in their assets. Based on this average, your company is doing pretty well, and you are within the ballpark. Yet still, you have room for improvement, and you need to capitalize on any and all opportunities. Your competitors are generating $0.32/per invested more than you are with their assets.

There is an opportunity to get more out of the equipment you have since your result is lower than the industry average. The next six ratios all deal with the Working Capital Cycle. The Working Capital Cycle is also referred to as the Cash Conversion Cycle and it tells you how fast money moves in your company. In other words, these ratios determine your organization's Speed of Cash and what needs to be done to enhance it.

Unlike when I was a Missouri State Trooper, the Speed of Cash is measured in days, not miles per hour. You use three components to measure speed: inventory accounts receivable, and accounts payable. You first calculate a turnover rate for each component. Then you convert it to a number of days.

REAL TALK: How Many Times of Year Do I Have to Replace Inventory That I've Sold?

Inventory Turnover Rate

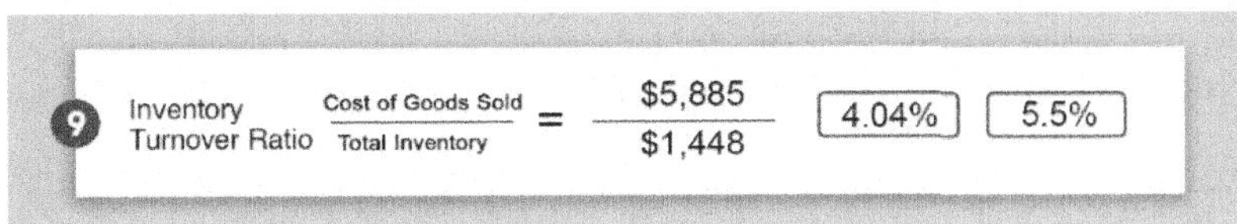

To put it simply, the Inventory Turnover Rate tells you how many times per year you are replacing inventory after selling it. To determine this ratio, you will need the total Cost of Goods Sold amount from the income statement. An important point to note here is that inventory is an asset in your Balance Sheet so long as it doesn't get sold. The minute the inventory gets sold in the market, it transforms into an expense in the Income Statement.

This specific expense is known as the Cost of Goods Sold. To calculate this ratio, you will need both the Cost of Goods along with the Total Inventory left on your shelf. As an example, we can take Cost of Goods Sold as $5,855 million and Total Inventory as $1,448 million. After dividing these two numbers, you will receive an Inventory Turnover Rate of 4.04.

This value is telling you that your company is replacing inventory a total of 4 times per year. In other words, you are selling and replacing your inventory at a speed of 4.04. Now, as always, to find out whether the turnover rate is good or bad, you will have to compare your Inventory Turnover Rate with the Industry Average. In this case, you can take the industry average as 5.5 from our sample industry averages sheet. This means that your competitors are replacing their inventories 5 times per year. In our example, it seems that your inventory is staying on your shelf much longer than the competition, which is a real opportunity to improve your cash flow. Just reduce the amount of inventory your carry. And, if you have any doubts that a lower turnover rate is worse for your cash flow, you can prove it through the next ratio.

REAL TALK: How Many Days Does A Piece of Inventory Sit on The Shelf Before Someone Buys It?

Inventory Days (DSI)

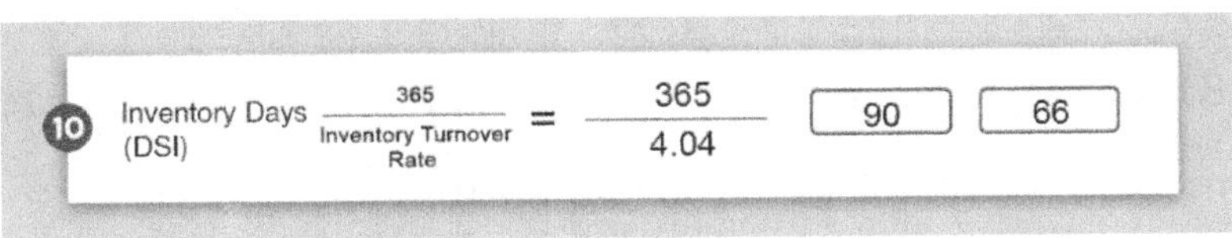

If you wish to find out just how long your inventory is staying on the shelf, you need to convert the turnover rate into days. The result of this ratio will describe the exact time your inventory is sitting on the shelf without earning a single dollar. The ratio is simple. Just divide 365 by the inventory turnover rate we calculated above. By using our example, we divide 365 (total number of days in 1 year)/ by 4.04 (Inventory Turnover Rate). The result is 90. Inventory sits on the shelf for 90 days. Makes sense, right? The turnover rate is 4 times per year or once per quarter. Now, you must ask yourself is this value good or bad? Well, we will follow the same protocol and compare it with the industry average.

Let's say that the industry average amounts to a total of just 66 days. In the case of Inventory Days (DSI), the lesser the time, the more efficient and productive your company is performing. This is mainly because the inventory on the shelf ties up the cash you might need to run your business. By having dead money on your shelf or factory, you are missing out on major earning opportunities.

That is why you want the inventory to replace faster and get converted as soon as humanly possible. For 90 days are longer than 66 days, it means that you have more dead money lying around in your company which could be used to fund the company's operation. In the end, these two ratios cover the first component of the Working Capital

Cycle. Talking about the remaining two components of the cycle Accounts Receivable and Accounts Payable, they also follow a similar calculation formulation like Inventory.

REAL TALK: How Many Times Per Year Do My Customers Pay Their Invoices in Full?

Accounts Receivable Turnover Rate

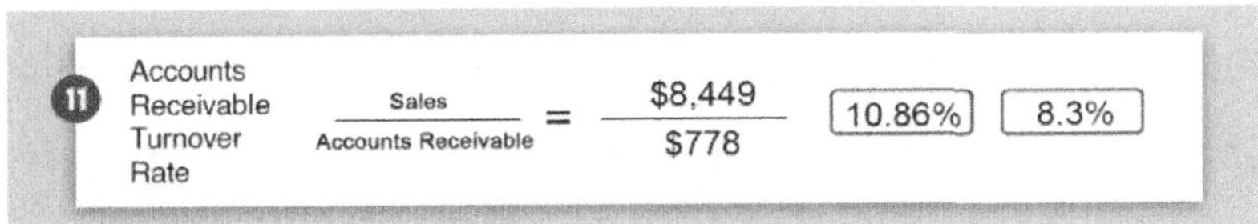

In the case of Accounts Receivable Turnover Rate, you calculate just how fast or swiftly your customers pay you for work you have performed. Or, in other words, how fast can you expect payment upon delivering the invoice to your clientele. To determine this ratio, you will divide your total number of sales with the amount your company is owed at the present moment. Our total sales will remain the same at $8,449 million and you can take the total amount owed currently (Accounts Receivable) as $778,000. When we divide these two numbers, we come to an Accounts Receivable Turnover Rate of 10.86. Let's suppose the industry average, in this case, is 8.3. Now, which is better? Many people get confused at this point as they don't know how to interpret this number. Let me simplify it for you, a higher AR turnover rate simply means that your company gets paid more often. At the same time, a higher turnover rate implies that the company is getting paid much faster. In our case, your company is performing way better than the competition. This is mainly because you are getting paid approximately 11 times per year while your competitors are receiving payments only 8 times a year. Now, to prove this result, you will need the following ratio.

REAL TALK: How Long Do I Have to Wait for My Customers to Pay Their Invoices?

AR Collection Period (DSO)

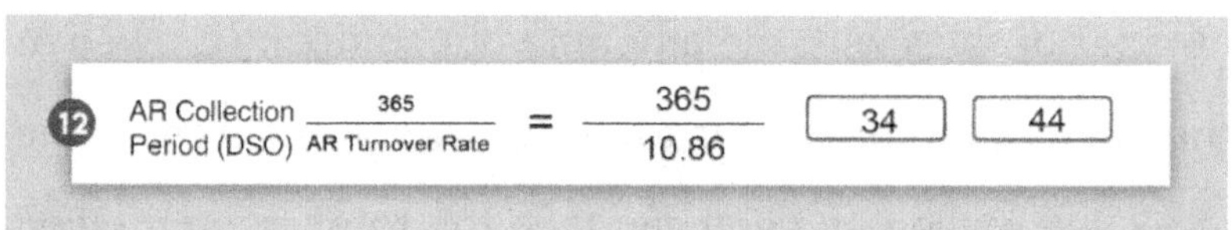

In realistic terms, the AR or Accounts Receivable Collection Period tells you, the entrepreneur, how fast you are getting paid in terms of days. To find out your AR

Collection Period, you will have to divide 365 by your AR Turnover Rate which is 10.86. So, 365/10.86 equals to 34 days. This is a really good number as it is extremely difficult to maintain a 30-day collection period. Most of the time, in order to sustain this AR Collection Period, you need to get your customers to pay cash up front. If we were to take the industry average of 44 days, this shows us that your company is faring better than the majority of your competition as they have to wait an additional 10 days for their payment. Most likely, you and your staff are good at collecting on your invoices.

However, you must also be aware that both Accounts Receivable and Accounts Payable can act as double-edged swords. This is mainly because it is possible to be too good or too weak in both collections and payments. What do I mean by this? I mean that if you pursue your collections aggressively, there is a fair chance that your clientele ends up turning toward your competitors, thereby decreasing your sales. In our example, your company is collecting your invoices very quickly. Your process might be too aggressive. Tell me if you would like this.

You are contacted by the company three days after you send the invoice. Then you get an email about 6 days later. Who knows maybe another phone call or a personal visit? If someone used this technique to get me to pay an invoice, I'd probably not do business with them again. So, there is such a thing as being too aggressive at collections. This situation could become frustrating for your consumers and they might switch to your competitor; a competitor who just sends their invoices and only contacts the customer in a 30 to 40-day period.

This is why you need to maintain a balance regarding both of these components. In my experience, your collection period needs to hover around the industry average. By maintaining the industry average, you are giving yourself room to maneuver your collections whenever the situation presents itself.

REAL TALK: How Many Times Per Year Do I Pay My Vendors Invoices in Full?

Accounts Payable Turnover Rate

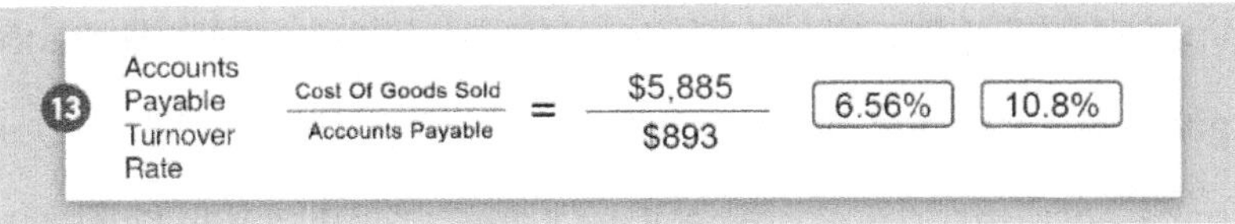

When we talk about accounts payable, we are focusing on how well you can pay your bills and obligations. This is why, when calculating the Accounts Payable Turnover Rate, you will have to factor in your Cost of Goods Sold, (which is money you are used to purchasing your inventory) and your present Accounts Payable (the money you owe to all vendors right now). Let's suppose our Cost of Goods Sold amounts to $5,855 million while Accounts Payable equals to $893,000. So, our Accounts Payable Turnover Rate will equal to $5,855 million/$893,000, or 6.5. This means that you pay your bills and obligations 6.5 times per year.

Now, again, is this Turnover Rate good or bad? Let us compare it with the industry average, which, in our example, is 10.8 times a year. Well, believe it or not, your company is doing better than the competition. This is mainly because paying slower or fewer times per year is far better for your overall cash flow. The reason why I am saying this is because, despite it being the money you owe, you are keeping the money in the company. We haven't given it away and because of this, the money is still in your bank account. Your competitors have already given the cash to their vendors.

Here is a side note. I am calculating only the Cost of Goods Sold number with the Accounts Payable amount. You can also include all Operating Expenses against all Accounts Payable if you are diligent about entering your bills into the accounting system regularly. Now let's convert the AP Turnover Rate into a number of days.

REAL TALK: How Long Do My Vendors Have to Wait for Me to Pay Their Invoices?

Accounts Payable Days (DPO)

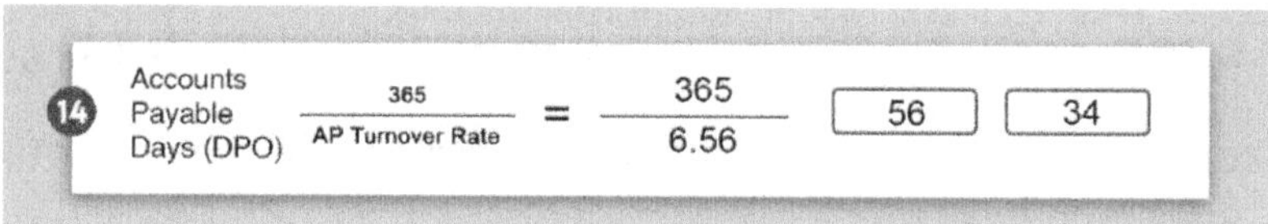

The Accounts Payable Days or DPO represents the total number of days you take to pay off your bills or financial obligations. So, after converting our Accounts Payable Rate into days, we will reach a result of 365/10.8=56 days. In other words, you are paying off your bills in 56 days while (after comparing it to the industry average) everyone else is paying their bills in 34 days. You are getting free money or interest-free credit from your vendors to the tune of about 22 days' worth.

However, in all honesty, this seemingly perfect situation can be a little touchy for your brand. This is mainly because your vendors are counting on you to make timely payments. If you don't fall under their expectations, you could suffer from many issues. These issues include poor pricing, no discounts, or even complete withdrawal. This is why, again, you need to maintain a balance and hover your accounts payable days around the industry average as well. Doing so puts you in an ideal position to negotiate with vendors if you need to.

This technique also enables you to solve short-term cash-flow problems before they turn into major issues. For example, you could hold onto an invoice a little longer on occasion if you run a little short on money one month. Can you see why writing this chapter was so tough? It is a painfully necessary step and believe it or not it is more fun to do it on a real company. I mean, c'mon. Telling you how to calculate ratios on a fake sample company is dreadfully boring. But now that we have TESTED our company, let's move to the second step of The Financial Doctor Method and ANALYZE the data we just collected.

Chapter 6
ANALYZE

You must be wondering why we went through the long ratio analysis exercise? Well, to put your mind at ease, let me say that your efforts and calculations are now about to pay off. This is because, in this chapter, we'll analyze and measure the financial impact of our tests and figure out whether or not the company has any hidden cash opportunities. This is awesome. We are about to turn ratios into dollars. I know that gets your attention.

Through these tests, you can tell how your company is leaking cash in any of the most common places hidden cash exists. By analyzing the financial impact, you can identify and develop a plan to capture the money you're currently leaving on the table by the way you operate your business.

This phase will describe the true picture of your business and how you can adjust your strategies and accounts to secure more money to fund your transferable value amount. The next step is as simple as performing six key calculations. These calculations will allow you to figure out the weaknesses and strengths of your company. And, because of this discernment, you will identify the known areas of earning additional cash and revenues. Let's take a look at the Financial Impact Worksheet to get started.

Hidden Cash Worksheet

Figure 6.1

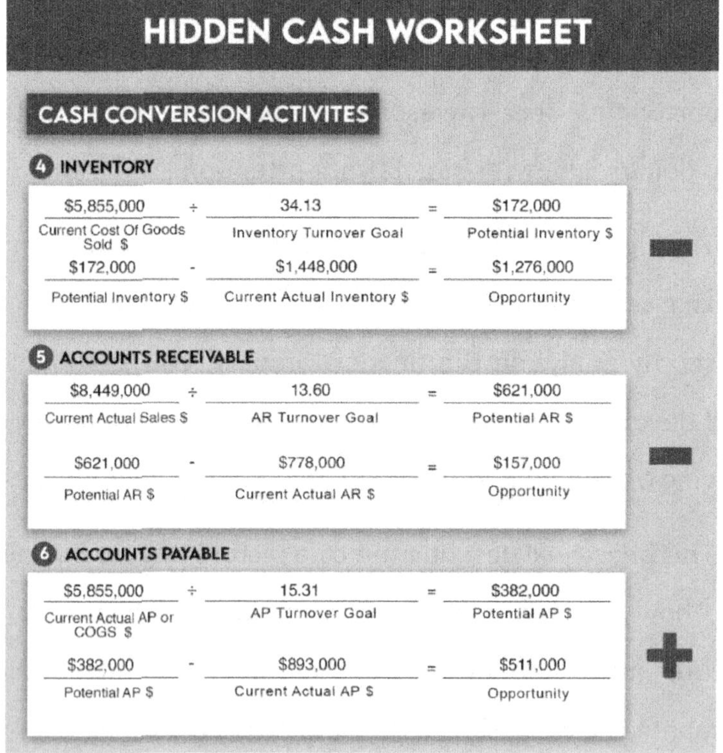

At first glance, you might notice a peculiar fact. This fact is that the Financial Impact Worksheet is divided into two parts. The first three calculations are focus on pure cash generation activities and the last three calculations revolve around the cash conversion activities of the business. Separating them on the Financial Impact Worksheet should help you understand the different "levers" you have to control cash moving through your business. It also helps us understand where to go to take advantage of the opportunities we find.

First of all, let's agree that when I talk about Financial Impact, I'm talking about the money you are leaving on the table by not performing as well as the industry average or your targets. We will be calculating what our business would look like if we performed like our competitors or achieved our company's goals.

Cash Generation Activities

Sales

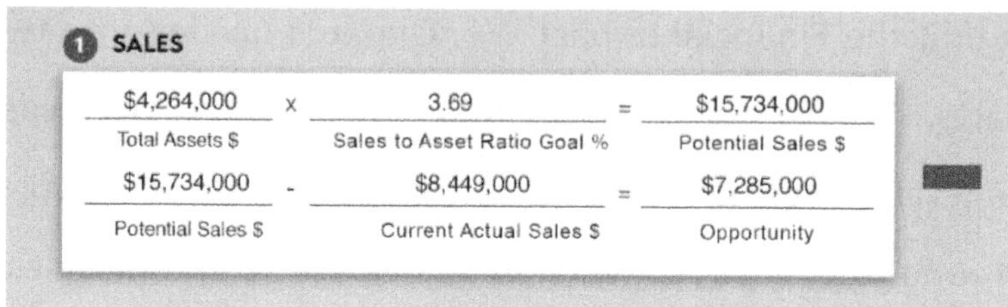

$4,264,000	x	3.69	=	$15,734,000
Total Assets $		Sales to Asset Ratio Goal %		Potential Sales $
$15,734,000	-	$8,449,000	=	$7,285,000
Potential Sales $		Current Actual Sales $		Opportunity

Out of the three cash-generating activities, the first and most complex is Sales. It's complex because it involves the use of the Sales to Assets ratio we calculated in the last chapter. Sales to assets is not a very commonly used ratio by the small business owner, but it can be super powerful if they understood it better. To find the financial impact of sales, we need to look at the Sales to Asset Ratio of our previous example.

This ratio tells you how much revenue your company is earning from every dollar you have invested in a piece of equipment. We are going to use the results of our Sales to Assets calculation to determine how much revenue we should be generating with the amount of equipment we have in our company. The calculation starts by looking at the balance sheet and identifying your company's total assets. Based on our sample company, the total assets equaled $4.3 million. For the second part of this calculation, you need to multiply this number by our target sales to asset turnover rate. In this case, we'll use the industry average. However, you might find that you are already better than the industry average and have a goal that you think you can achieve. I mean, who wants to be average when you can be exceptional!

One of the ways I like to use the sales to asset ratio is to determine how much additional revenue I can expect from a new equipment purchase. Most small businesses just kind of guess at how much they can grow. You can use this ratio to come up with a more realistic number based on how you currently use your equipment. The sales to asset ratio in our sample company are 1.98. So, if they invested $100,000 in a new piece of equipment, they could expect it to produce an additional $198,000 in revenue ($100,000 x 1.98). In our example, the industry average is 2.3. Now, you need to multiply your total assets with the industry average, and you will come to the result of $4.3 million x 2.3 = $9.9 million. When you subtract this amount with the original or actual sales, which were $8.4 million, you will get a result of.

$9.9 million - $8.4 million = $1.5 million Financial Impact.

What does this amount tell us? This result is showing one of two things. The first sign is that the average company in our industry generates $1.5 million more than our sample company. And the second clue is that our sample company has enough equipment to generate $9.9 million in sales, adding no more equipment. However, this is only possible if the company operates efficiently and makes sales smoothly and methodically.

You can also say that there is a hidden selling opportunity available to the company without having to add any additional equipment or machinery. You have successfully found a hidden cash opportunity worth $1.5 million! Although achieving this is easier said than done. Usually increasing sales in one of the hardest things to do, so I usually try to take advantage of the other hidden cash opportunities first. But it is super helpful to know that the opportunity is present. After improving on every other area, you can focus on sales to grow the sample company. More importantly, you can sell more without making any more investment in the company. Just sell baby!

Gross Profit

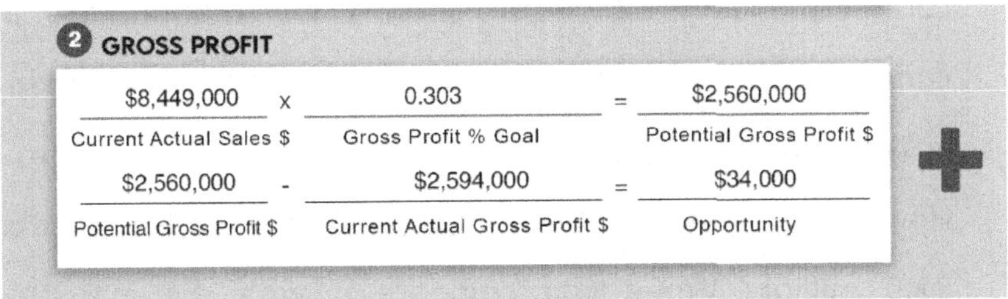

2 GROSS PROFIT

$8,449,000	x	0.303	=	$2,560,000
Current Actual Sales $		Gross Profit % Goal		Potential Gross Profit $
$2,560,000	-	$2,594,000	=	$34,000
Potential Gross Profit $		Current Actual Gross Profit $		Opportunity

Now it's time to dig into my favorite and most prominent cash-generating activity, which is gross profit. Gross Profit is the most important number on your income statement because it is the ONLY place you can generate cash to run your business and contribute to your transferable value. If you just said to yourself that you could also sell some assets and get some cash; you're being a D.U.M.B. business owner.

If you sell your assets, then you also reduce your ability to generate revenue, see above. So, to calculate the financial impact of Gross Profit, you will need the actual sales of our sample company. In this case, the actual sales equaled $8.4 million. After finding this value, you need to ask yourself what the gross profit percentage goal of the sample company is. This goal is not what the sample company is earning. It is the goal or industry average which the sample company wants to achieve. The average company makes 32.2% of Gross Profit Margin. So, a company with sales of $8.4 million will earn $2.7 million in gross profit. ($8.4 million*32.2% = $2.688 or $2.7 million). However, in actuality, the sample company made close to $2.6 million. When you compare it with the industry average, you will come to a result of $2.7 million-$2.6 million= $100,000 in financial impact. This value shows that there is a $100,000 difference between the company's potential and actual profitability.

Remember in the last chapter when we determined that the difference between our performance and the industry average was about 1%? The gross profit margin of the sample company was 30.8%, while the industry average was 32.2%. That 1% now has a different meaning. Judging from the results we calculated, you have proof that a difference of 1% equals an additional $100,000 in gross profit for the sample company. Think about that. A 1%

increase in gross profit will put an additional $100,000 in your pocket since we are already covering our operating expenses! Now, the main point to ponder in this situation is how will the sample company acquire the additional 1%? There are many ways to increase the company's gross profit. You could call up your vendors and ask for a 15% haircut or drop in prices. Obviously, the vendor will refuse your request and will respond with a counteroffer of maybe 5%. Since you only need 1% to get a $100,000 increase, you can accept the vendor's proposal and earn tremendously from the re-negotiated pricing. Similar to this strategy, there are a plethora of techniques that can amplify your company's profitability.

Net Profit before Tax

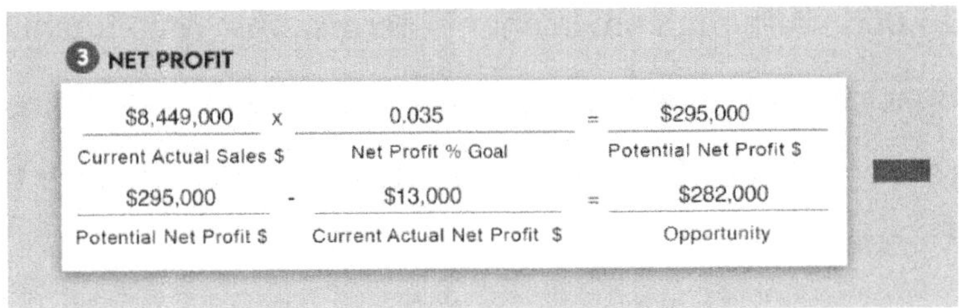

By now, you have already learned that the sample company is not making a lot of money. However, you still don't know how much the company is losing in the opportunity to capture REAL DOLLARS. To determine this, you need to calculate the third and last cash-generating activity, Net profit Before Tax. Much like the above two cash-generating activities, you need certain values for your calculation. We are going to start with our current sales volume again. The total sales of the sample company are $8.4 million. Then, you will need the industry average, which, in our case, is 3.1%. If your company was an average company, it would make 3.1% in Net Profit before Tax.

In cash terms, the Pre-Tax target Profit would be 3.1%*$8.4 million= $252,000. This is a lot better than the actual net profit before tax the sample company made of $13,000. Although in layman's terms, the real financial impact of the sample company would be $239,000 (Target Pre-Tax Profit of $252,000 -the actual Net Profit before tax $13,000= $239,000).

Now, you might remember that net profit before tax is by default a result. That means you can't do anything to net profit to change it. You will need to make changes in the gross profit earned and operating expense spent to capture the $239,000. That being the case, an average company would already have an additional $100,000 in gross profit, so they would have to cut an additional $139,000 in operating expenses.

By definition, the operating expense of a company is the difference between gross profit and net profit before taxation. $239,000-$100,000= $139,000. So, if you were to read between the lines, you notice that for the company to match the industry average, it NEEDS to cut $139,000 in operating expenses. What I like about this technique is that the corrective actions just jump off the page. I don't need to spend hours analyzing my financial statements to formulate a plan. These calculations will point you in the right direction every time.

What we learned is that the sample company is falling behind in all three cash-generating activities; Sales, Gross Profit, and Net Profit before Tax, and there are great opportunities available to increase money within the organization.

PRO-TIP – I always put a + or a – sign next to the financial impact amount on the worksheet. In this case, I would use a minus sign by sales, gross profit, and net profit, because the situation was worse than the target in all three categories. If my performance was better, I would use the plus sign. You'll see why this is helpful when we build the Cash Leak Map at the end of this chapter.

Cash Conversion Activities

With Cash Conversion Activities, we are basically evaluating how efficient your company is at converting its assets into cash. Similar to Cash Generation Activities, cash conversion also has three main components. These three components include Inventory, Accounts Receivable, and Accounts Payable. Once you calculate these three components (I sometimes call these levers), you will have a clear idea of how which lever I need to pull to capture any hidden cash opportunities that exist in my company's cash conversion cycle processes.

Inventory

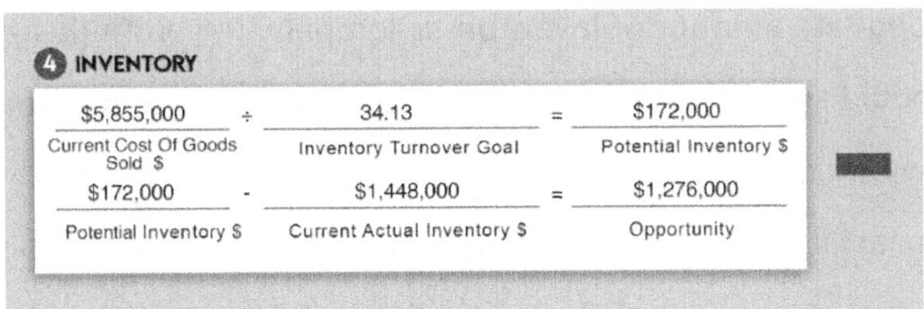

Let's begin where the cash conversion activities begin with the purchase of inventory. What we are trying to determine with this calculation is how much inventory we should have on the shelf compared to the average company or our turn-over goal. When we are calculating the desired inventory amount, the first thing you will need is the Cost of Goods Sold amount from the income statement.

With our sample company, the Cost of Goods Sold amounted to $5.855 million. By dividing the Cost of Goods Sold amount by the average turnover rate of the industry (5.5), we find out that our sample company should have $1.065 million ($5.855 million/5.5 times) worth of inventory. Now, this number is highly significant as no one ever tells you the ideal inventory a company needs to have on their shelf. Through this calculation, you can find this vital number and figure out what the market feels is an adequate amount of inventory a company in your industry should have on the shelf. In our sample, the actual inventory amounts to $1.448 million. If we were to find the financial impact of the company's inventory, we would arrive at a result of $1.448-$1.065= $383,000. Now, you must think, what does this value mean? This value means that the sample company has $383,000 worth of extra inventory on its shelf. It means that you should have $1.065 million but you have $1.448. That is $383,000 too much.

If you, were to reduce the sample company's inventory to $1.065 million, the company will put $383,000 directly in their pocket. I know your first question would be, how is this possible, Mike? Well, it is possible because of one basic reason. This reason is that the money the sample company would have spent in replenishing or replacing the inventory will instead stay in the bank. By not replacing the inventory, you will save nearly $400,000 and keep that amount in the company, not give it to your vendors. This also means that the sample company has $383,000 worth of hidden cash opportunities and is performing negatively, much like the rest of the activities mentioned above. Therefore, I'd mark the inventory calculation with a minus sign to show I was worse than I wanted to be. Implying that I have too much inventory.

The next two calculations are interesting. When we did the ratio analysis in the previous chapter, I got a feeling that the sample company was pretty good at collecting from their customers and paying their vendors.

Accounts Receivable

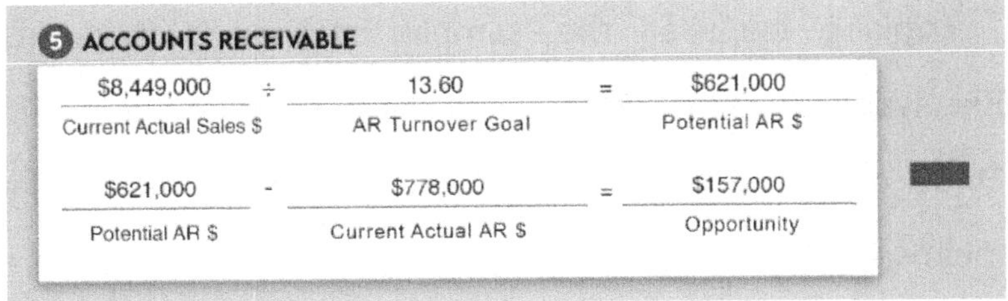

After buying your inventory, hopefully, you sell it. If you don't collect cash at the time of the sale, then you might have given the customer an invoice to pay. The thing about giving someone an invoice is you have to wait until they pay. This is considered to be your Accounts Receivable. Accounts receivable is nothing, but the money owed to us by our clientele, and it acts as an asset in the Balance Sheet. In this calculation, we are going to figure out how much the average company is owed based on our sample company's level of sales. To calculate this number, you will need the total sales of the sample company, $8.449 million. Now, as always, you must consider the industry average or Target Accounts Receivable Turnover Rate. The Target Accounts Receivable tells you how many times the competition is getting paid each year. So, the industry average for the sample company is 8.3 or 8 times per year.

Looking back at the sample company's Accounts Receivable Turnover Rate, the sample company was paid 10.86 or 11 times per year by its consumer base. That means they were better than average. They got paid more often. Here is how much they would be owed if they only collected 8 times per year. The average company would be waiting for their customers to pay $1.024 million ($8.499 / 8 times= $1.024 million). However, in reality, the sample company is owed only $778,000. The financial impact or difference between the industry average and the sample company's Accounts Receivable is $246,000 ($1.024 million

-$778,000= $246,000). The sample company is already doing better than the competition. This calculation proves that the sample company is owed less than the average companies in the industry. You can also say that the sample company bought in, over the year, an additional $246,000 in Accounts Receivable, making the company BETTER than its competition. For this reason, I would put a plus sign next to the Accounts Payable calculation.

Accounts Payable

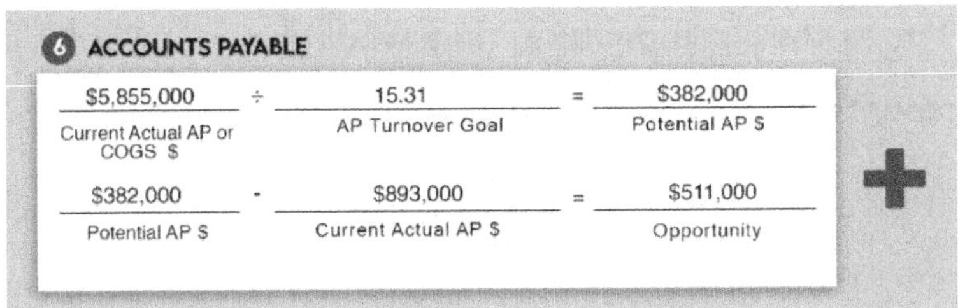

In the previous calculations, we were determining how long it takes for a dollar to come back to the company after a company buys and pays an invoice. This is evaluating the speed of cash inflows into the company. This calculation about Accounts Payable is calculating how fast the sample company has money moving out of the organization.

To calculate the financial impact of Accounts Payable., you need to divide the Cost of Goods Sold with the Accounts Payable Goal or industry average Accounts Payable Turnover Rate. With our sample company, the Cost of Goods Sold of the sample company equals $5.855 million, all the while the Industry Average amounts to 10.8 or 11 times per year. After dividing these two values, the target Accounts Payable in dollars would be $5.855 million/10.8= $542,000. This is the amount the sample company should ideally owe to its vendors if it were average. If they paid as often as their competitors, they would have $542,000 in Accounts Payable on the balance sheet.

However, looking at our sample company's balance sheet, the company owes $893,000 to its vendors and suppliers. If we were to convert this difference on a Cash basis, you would conclude $542,000 - $893,000 = $-351,000 Financial Impact. You might ask yourself, is this value good or bad? Well, the result came in negative so it must be bad for the company, right? Well, wrong, this is another strength for our sample company. Why is that? The simple answer is that even though the sample company owes

$351,000, the money has still not left the organization. The sample company has $351,000 at its disposal, and they can use this money as they wish. As compared to the sample company, the average company or competitor has already spent their money by paying off their bills and obligations to the vendor. If you are having any doubts regarding this value, you can view the additional amount as a source of cash for the sample company. This is mainly because an increase in liability from a banker's perspective is a Source of Cash. The money is present in the company, and it will stay with the company until the owner pays off their liability.

It doesn't mean they don't owe it, it just means that they haven't spent the money and should still have it in cash flow. It may seem weird but paying your bills a little slower is a good thing if you can do it, so I would use a plus sign here to indicate we are better than our competitors here. You might be relieved to know that the bulk of the math needed to evaluate your company is DONE! I don't blame you if you just skimmed over the math parts. I take it as a compliment. You trust me to tell you the right thing.

Besides, this isn't a math textbook, this book is designed to teach you concepts and techniques to use on your own company. I bet those numbers will excite you. With this calculation, we have come to the end of the rigorous and grueling analysis stage. I know it was difficult and tedious, but you can find solace in knowing that we have successfully completed the second step of The Financial Doctor Method. We have calculated the six key components of the Cash Conversion and the Cash Generation activities in your company to uncover any cash opportunities that were hidden inside the sample company's operations. Now, that we have TESTED and ANALYZED the sample company, we are finally able to move towards the third step, DIAGNOSIS.

During the DIAGNOSIS step, you will look at the issues you have found in the first two steps. When a doctor looks at your symptoms, they are trying to point to the overall ailment you have so they can prescribe TREATMENT. After all, a runny nose and a fever are just symptoms of an ailment which might be the flu, or it could be coronavirus. During the DIAGNOSE step, we will learn how to build the Cash Leak Map and figure out the root cause behind the sample company's problems. That way, we can develop an action plan to put this company back on the right foot.

Chapter 7
DIAGNOSE

So far, we have a ton of information on our sample company. Just like a doctor, we now have the results of our analysis and can make a diagnosis. Believe it or not, when you look at the results of the test, they will point directly towards the root cause of the problems within your company.

So far, we have done a thorough analysis by testing the major "organs" or components, of our sample company's financial statements. We then analyzed the results of those tests to understand which "organs," or components, of the sample company are not functioning properly. Now we are at the diagnosis phase of this process.

After doing the detailed analysis of the sample company, we can see the money leaking out of our sample business. We know that they lack in many areas compared to their competitors, especially in cash-generating activities. However, just knowing that they are underperforming is not enough to solve the issue. You have to dig a little deeper to find out the root cause of these problems. By identifying the root cause, you can address the real problem and understand the cause and effect relationship that everything has in your business.

For this purpose, the first thing we need to do is create a Cash Leak Map. You've got to be asking yourself what a cash leak map is. A cash leak map basically gives you a quick picture of your business' performance compared to the industry average, or your specific business goals. In reality, it's a really simple and easy way to look at the results of your analysis in the last step. If you're like me, pictures tend to help me understand things a lot better. I have incorporated this map below to make things easy to understand.

Figure 7.1

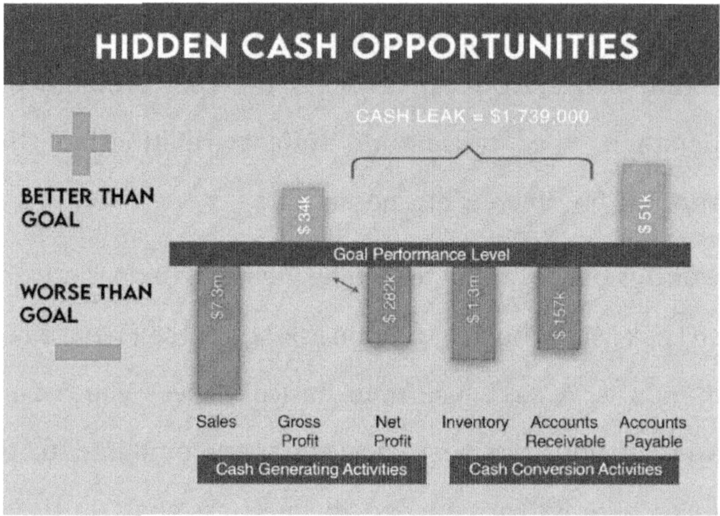

So, as you can see that the first and the most prominent thing on the cash leak map is a Goal Performance Line. We can also call it a Zero Line. A goal performance line is just like the surface of the Earth. You know, because treasures are hidden right beneath it. The goal performance line is used to create a visual aid to see where you have opportunities. If your company is performing better than your goal, you land above the goal performance line. On the contrary, if the performance of your business is worse than your expectations, you fall below the goal performance line. This line helps you find your hidden cash opportunities because we are looking for items below the surface. So, let's take a look at the essential figures from the last chapter to understand our cash leak map.

Cash Generating Activities

We have three elements in cash-generating activities. These are;

1. Sales
2. Gross Profit
3. Net Profit

In the previous chapter, we identified that the financial impact of our sales effort was $1.5 million. We determined this because our sales to assets ratio were lower than the industry average. The average is $2.30 per dollar invested and our sample company only yields $1.90. The net difference was $1.5 million in an additional sales opportunity. It signifies that our sample company is not generating enough sales. So, on the cash leak map, the amount should fall below the goal performance line. Hence, we will draw a red line on our cash leak map.

Similarly, the gross profit margin of our sample company is 30.8%, whereas the industry average is 32.2%. Though we are only 1% behind the industry average, it is still worse than that of the competitor. The financial impact of our sample company performing 1% less than the industry average resulting in a hidden cash opportunity of about $100,000. TO indicate that it is another place we can get cash in this company, we place another red line below the goal performance line.

According to the industry average, the sample company should generate the net profit before tax of $252,000. However, at present, it is only making $13,000. So, the company is way behind its competitors in the industry. To the tune of about $239,000. Here is another hidden cash opportunity we can take advantage of by increasing gross profit and cutting expenses. Remember, net profit is just a result. You need to make changes in the other components to see the benefit. Hence, we will draw another red line below the goal performance line. In terms of all the cash-generating activities, the sample company is underperforming. There can be multiple reasons behind it.

If we talk about the sales volume of the sample company, it is quite lower than the industry average. Its sales to asset ratio are 1.98 which means it generates $1.98 against each dollar invested. Whereas the industry average is 2.3, which signifies that the sample company should at least generate $2.3 against each dollar invested. If the return on assets percentage is lower than the industry average, it indicates an inefficient use of company facilities such as machinery or fleet.

For example, the company may own too many fleet vehicles that spend more time sitting in parking lots than hauling manufactured goods. Another possibility is that their production equipment isn't being used to its fullest capacity. Long-term or capital leases that cost more per square foot than the company yields in sales per square foot are another example of inefficient use of company assets. Though this is an alarming situation, multiple solutions exist to solve this issue that we will discuss in the. The second element is gross profit. It is extremely important for maintaining the profitability of any business. Even a slight variation in the gross profit margin can have a large impact on the net profit. In our case, the gross profit margin of the sample is also lower than the industry average. However, the situation is quite better in this case because the sample company needs only 1% of additional gross profit to match the industry average.

The possible causes of low gross profit margin are

- Poor pricing
- Poor buying
- Poor product mix
- Poor productivity
- Spoilage and shrinkage

Other common reasons behind low gross profit can be a decrease in selling price without any decrease in the cost of goods sold. Or it can be due to an increase in the cost of goods sold without an increase in the selling price. Similarly, when you order too much inventory relative to demand, you normally have to discount the remaining inventory to generate revenue and cash flow. As a result, your gross profit declines. The good news is all of these can be corrected or improved!

Much like sales and gross profit, the company is not performing well in terms of net profit before tax as well. Makes sense, right? After all, if we are bringing less money into the company, chances are high that we wouldn't be keeping that much at the end of the period. According to the industry average, our company is supposed to make 3.1% in net profit. However, currently, we are way behind this percentage.

The two main causes of low net profit margin are

- Low gross profit margin – the money you have to spend.
- Too high overhead cost – the way you spend it.

Yes, we have a low gross profit margin, but here, a larger reason is high operating expenses. An increase in operating expenses means less profit for a business. If your net profit margin is lower than the industry average, you need to take serious actions to control your operating expenses.

How much should you cut? The easiest way to find out is to subtract your gross profit cash opportunity ($100k) from your net profit opportunity ($239k). Our sample company should cut $139,000 in operating expenses this year. In the next chapter, I will share various ways that can help you reduce your operating expenses and improve your net profit before tax.

Now that we have diagnosed the problems in the sample company's cash-generating activities, we will move on to the next step, which is the diagnosis of their cash conversion activities. Similar to cash generation activities, cash conversion activities also comprise of three elements that I call levers.

These levers are:

1. Inventory
2. Accounts Receivable
3. Accounts Payable

Following the same logic as above, we'll first look at how this company does with inventory management. In chapter 6, we identified that a company our size would have about $1.065 million worth of inventory on their shelf. However, the actual amount of inventory our sample company has is $1.448 million. It means the sample company has an extra, or we should say an unnecessary inventory of $383,000. This extra amount could have been used in something else that could generate more income. Looking back at the diagnosis section of cash-generating activities, we discussed that one of the possible causes of low gross profit margin is unnecessary inventory. So here, we got to know that we are starting to dial in our diagnosis.

Now let's get back to the main point of this section. Since the extra inventory leads to inefficient performance, this component also falls below the goal performance line. One of the major causes of the waste of inventory is a lack of market understanding. When companies don't give due importance to market research about customer demand and trends, they end up with too much inventory on their shelves.

Obviously, one of the best solutions to avoid this problem is thorough market research. I don't want to have to say it, but this is an area where the business owner looks D.U.M.B. By now, you understand that the sample company is not performing quite well. But surprisingly, in the next two components, the company's performance is above the industry average. Meaning, they are doing better than expected. The industry average for accounts receivable turnover is 8.3. However, the sample company's accounts receivable turnover is 10.86 or 11 times per year, which is excellent. When we convert that to dollars, that means our competitors would be waiting for customers to pay about $1.024 million, when we are only waiting on $778,000. It means you will have fewer accounts receivables on your balance sheet. And a low accounts receivable indicates a better cash inflow. So here, the sample company lands above the goal performance line. Now is the time to draw a green line above the Zero Line, for the amount of $264,000.

Obviously, we couldn't find any problem with this component, so just keep doing what you're doing. But be careful, if you are too aggressive with your collection processes, you could lose customers and sales. Now comes the third but the most interesting and tricky component, i.e., Accounts Payable. In the last chapter, we identified that the industry average for accounts payable turnover is 10.8. It means that your competitor pays their bills to their suppliers and vendors 11 times a year. The Cost of Goods

Sold of the sample company is $5.855 million. By dividing it by 10.8, we get $542,000. This is the amount that the sample company should ideally have on its accounts payable. However, the actual accounts payable of the sample company is $893,000. Now, most people get confused while analyzing this ratio. They don't understand whether or not having an amount more than the industry is good. So, if you are one of those people, I am here to clear the confusion. I know you owe more than you should. However, you actually will have a more positive impact on cash flow this way. Obviously, you will have to pay your vendors, but the longer you hold it, the better it is. While your competitors have already paid their bills and money has left the company, you still have the cash in your account. In fact, the green line we will draw above the goal performance line is for an additional $351,000.

Being able to stretch your payables is a double-edged sword. Although it indicates that your vendors trust you, and you have maintained a good relationship with them. Taking too much advantage of their generosity could hurt your business relationship and your wallet. As I said, performing better than your competitors in this category is indeed a competitive advantage for you. Nevertheless, you must sustain your vendor relationships, in the long run, to hold onto your advantage.

Now that we can visualize where the hidden cash opportunities are, let's look at how the components of your business are interconnected. We want to understand that by creating a solution for one component, we are unintentionally hurting another.

Below is the Root Cause Analysis chart.

Figure 7.2

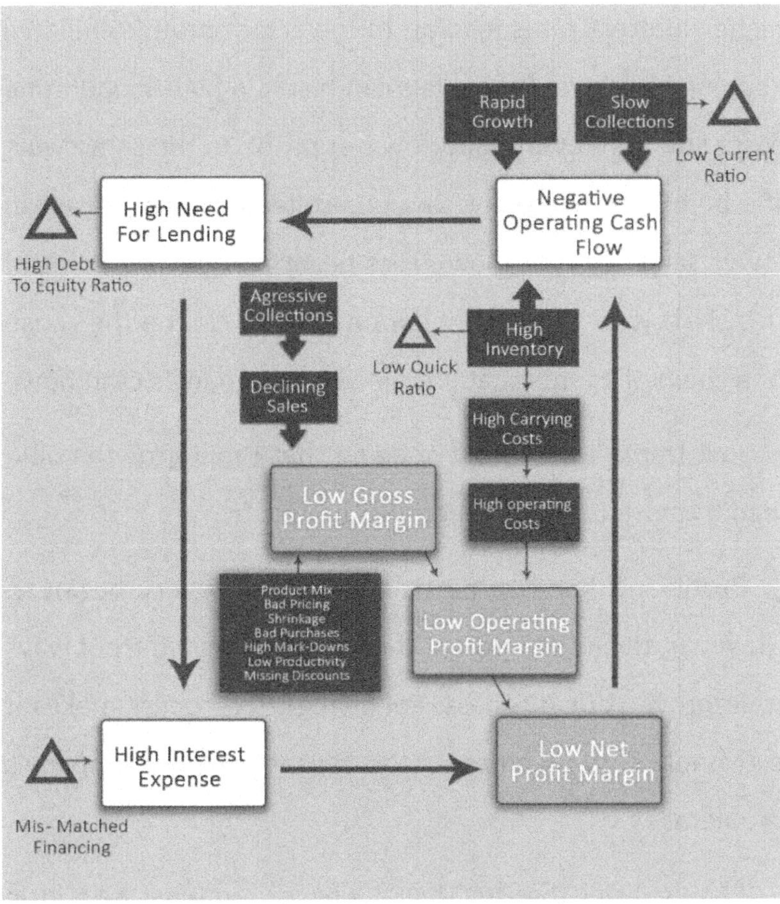

The arrows show different causes of low net profit. Let's start with negative operating cash flow. This one symptom is usually followed by a higher need for borrowing by the company because cash becomes tight. When they borrow there is the opportunity to mis-finance the asset or pay higher interest rates leading to lower net profit. Similarly, keeping high inventory levels can result in higher operating costs and then eventually, low net profit. In the same way, the being too aggressive in your collections may result in lower sales and then low gross profit margin The point of this chart is to show you how one action can be the cause of a chain of events that cripple your company's cash flow.

Just think, who would imagine that rapid growth could lead to more borrowing and less net profit?

Profit and loss are part and parcel of every business. However, the good news is, there are always different ways to improve your business. Following this process makes it extremely easy to pinpoint the causes of your company's problems.

I know, after the DIAGNOSIS phase, you must be a little anxious. But believe me, you don't need to worry. The process, worksheets, and templates are here to guide you. Once you understand what is causing the problems you can craft solutions that make the biggest impact without causing more harm. After all, a doctor's oath is to "Do No Harm."

By now we should be able to describe the problem areas of our business and start to formulate a course of action. Now let's move into the TREATMENT phase. We have a lot to discuss with the financial health of our sample company. On the bright side, we found several opportunities to turn this company around quickly.

Chapter 8
TREAT

We have been discussing the problems of the sample company over the last three chapters now. So, if you're like me, when I'm sick, I just want to get well. I feel the same way about companies. Let's just find the treatment of what is causing the problems. The good news is this chapter is entirely dedicated to treatment only. In the previous chapter, we found out five critical issues in the sample company's performance, along with a whole host of other problems that these issues created.

Here is a list of the 5 main issues, and the issues they cause within our sample company.

Figure 8.1

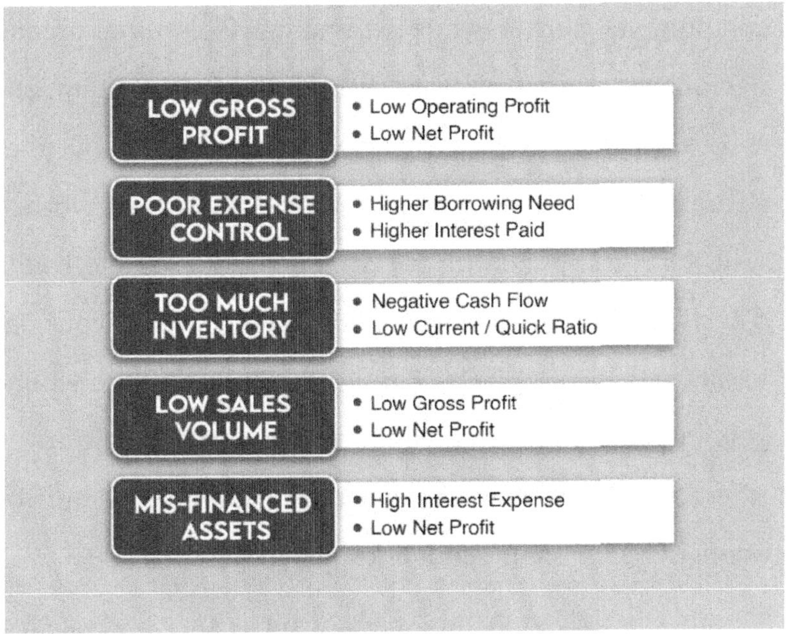

For every disease, there are several treatments. To identify the best-suited treatment for a patient, a physician first has to find out the root cause of the problem. Once the root cause is identified, treatment becomes easier. The whole last chapter gave you the tools to discover the root causes of your company's financial woes.

You need to understand that everything in your business is connected. Every business activity creates a ripple effect on other components. Let's understand it by just thinking about our bodies. Your body comprises of different components, such as your external parts, internal organs, nervous system, respiratory system, digestive system, and so forth. These components may seem different, but they all are connected. If one of your components is not working well, it affects your entire performance. For example, if your digestive system is disturbed, you can't focus on your day to day activities well. Or, if you are injured and the wound gets infected your body fights back by producing a fever. Now you not only have the pain of the initial injury, but you are fighting off an infection internally.

In the previous chapter, we created a root cause analysis map to analyze the causes and effects of the problems of the sample company. Based on the results, let's discuss some possible solutions.

A physician first has to diagnose the disease based on the patient's symptoms and then apply the treatment method that seems to be best-suited. So just like that, we will also discuss all the possible treatments which will not only treat the sample company but will also be helpful for any business you are currently running or planning to buy.

Low Gross Profit Margin

Here was something cool we discovered about the sample company in the last chapter. They only need to increase its gross profit by 1% to meet the industry average. Which by the way is worth about $100,000! However, the question is, how will they do it? Is there a magic wand they can wave to make everything perfect? Obviously not. There is no magic solution. You have to work hard to solve your business problems. Half of the battle is knowing where to look to start making changes and then getting started. Don't worry. This chapter will help you get started. So below are a few possible solutions that can help you improve the gross profit of your company.

Review Your Gross Profit Margin

You know that the gross profit of your business is lower than the industry average. If you are already better than the industry average, then compare yourself to your best year. The time when you felt like everything was running right. However, to get a clear picture, you must narrow it down. Analyze the gross profit of every product, service, and business division. After all, you might have some "losers" in your product mix that is dragging your overall average down. It happened to me in the restaurants. I loved serving chicken wings, but my pricing was so off that I might as well gave the customer a basket of wings and a $1 every time they ordered. Losing a $1 on every order sure does add up fast during football season!

How will it benefit you?

This will help you in two ways. First, you will get to know which product, service, or business division is the root cause of a low gross profit margin. Secondly, you will get to know about the most revenue-generating product, service, or business division. So, what's the next step now?

If you don't know where to start, check out my website and download the free Excel Inventory Master Template.

Figure 8.2

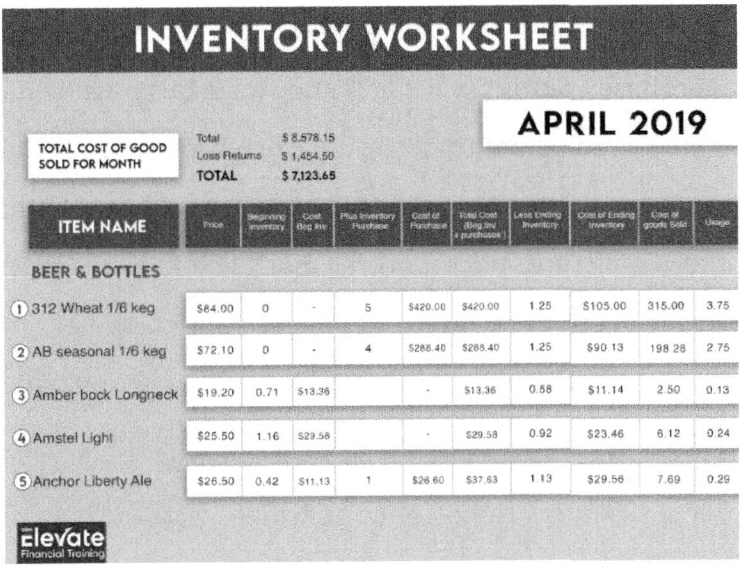

INVENTORY WORKSHEET

APRIL 2019

TOTAL COST OF GOOD SOLD FOR MONTH

Total	$ 8,578.15
Loss Returns	$ 1,454.50
TOTAL	**$ 7,123.65**

ITEM NAME	Price	Beginning Inventory	Cost Beg Inv	Plus Inventory Purchase	Cost of Purchase	Total Cost (Beg Inv + purchases)	Less Ending Inventory	Cost of Ending Inventory	Cost of goods Sold	Usage
BEER & BOTTLES										
(1) 312 Wheat 1/6 keg	$84.00	0	-	5	$420.00	$420.00	1.25	$105.00	315.00	3.75
(2) AB seasonal 1/6 keg	$72.10	0	-	4	$288.40	$288.40	1.25	$90.13	198.28	2.75
(3) Amber bock Longneck	$19.20	0.71	$13.36		-	$13.36	0.58	$11.14	2.50	0.13
(4) Amstel Light	$25.50	1.16	$29.58		-	$29.58	0.92	$23.46	6.12	0.24
(5) Anchor Liberty Ale	$26.50	0.42	$11.13	1	$26.60	$37.63	1.13	$29.56	7.69	0.29

Elevate Financial Training

http://www.cashflowmike.com

Once you see what is happening on a per-item basis, you can stop selling low margin lines and focus on the ones that work.

Increase Prices

Oftentimes, gross profit reduces because of an increase in the cost of goods sold. There can be multiple reasons for that. Such as you changed your vendor, or the existing vendor increased the price of the product your buying.

Whatever the reason is, when your cost increases, you have to increase prices as well, otherwise, you will have to compromise your gross profit. I know as a business owner; you may be reluctant to raise your price because you might lose some customers. However, you must understand that in the big picture, price doesn't matter in fact, there is a buyer at every price point. Retaining your customers has more to do with having a value proposition as I outlined in Chapter 1.

All customers are not price sensitive. Instead, they are focused on quality and value addition. Therefore, differentiate yourself in other ways, whether by giving superior value, going the extra mile, or reducing all the other (non-monetary) costs of doing business with you, such as effort, time, anxiety, and emotional costs.

Don't Offer Discounts

Offering discounts to your customers can be a great way to boost sales or retain long term customers. However, at times, discounting can be the death of your business. You don't realize it, but even a small discount can destroy your margins by a great deal. For example, if your gross profit margin is 50% and you offer a discount of 10% to your customers, you will need a 27% increase in your sales just to stand still. So, it's better to avoid giving any discounts to improve your company's efficiency.

Figure 8.3

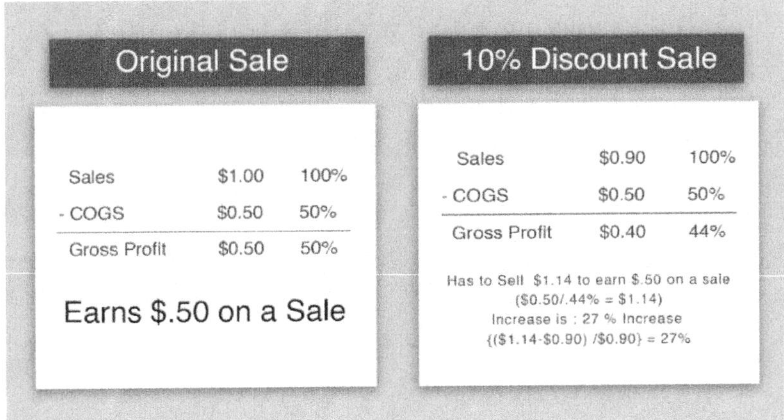

Reduce Production Cost

Reducing production costs can be one of the best ways to increase your margins. Now the question pops up how to reduce production cost. So again, I am here to help you. Just answer these questions.

- Are you getting the most out of your production equipment?
- Is your production machinery too old?
- Do you often have to spend a huge amount on repairs and maintenance?

Based on the answers to these questions, you can consider replacing an old asset. Or you can use your asset to its maximum capacity. This way, you can produce more units, and hence per unit cost will be reduced. Track and measure how productive your processes are running. You might find out that you have room to grow!

Other than the above three methods, here are a few more things to consider.

See if your vendors will give you cash discounts. It is normally a much better deal than delaying your payments.

✓ Monitor your inventory closely. You can use a good inventory management software to keep track of your inventory or use the items on hand formula below to set a more accurate amount of each item you carry. Producing too much or too little inventory can affect your margins. By using a proper inventory control system, you know exactly how much each of your products cost you without wading through old purchase invoices. It's easy, and it works well. Increasing your margins is all about making the most of what you sell right now. Here are the items on hand formula to help with this control. And, of course, this is also listed in the free Inventory Master Excel Template on my website. http://www.cashflowmike.com

Items on Hand = Amount Sold Per Month / # of deliveries in a month + a safety amount

Poor Expense Control

In the last chapter, we identified that the net profit margin of our sample company is way lower than the industry average. Obviously, one of the main reasons is the low amount of gross profit margin. However, another noteworthy reason is a high overhead cost. What does it mean? It signifies that we are not controlling our expenses efficiently. The proof was in the Expense Control calculation in The Home Run Financial System. The change in operating expenses should mirror the change in gross profit. Based on this calculation we determined that the sample company should cut about $100,000 in operating expenses.

So, what should they do? Here are a few key areas to look at.

Payroll

Take a look at the number of employees that are working for your business. Are they all working to their maximum capacity? Do you think laying off some of them will affect your business? Based on the answers to these questions, you can identify how much workforce you actually need. If three employees are performing tasks that two employees can do, you may have to let one go. However, in doing so, remember that trying to increase efficiency in this way can lead to a lower quality of work. So always be extra cautious while laying off or increasing the responsibility of your employees. It is best to find a mathematical method to help you determine your business headcount.

Here are two calculations to help you "right size" your team.

Figure 8.4

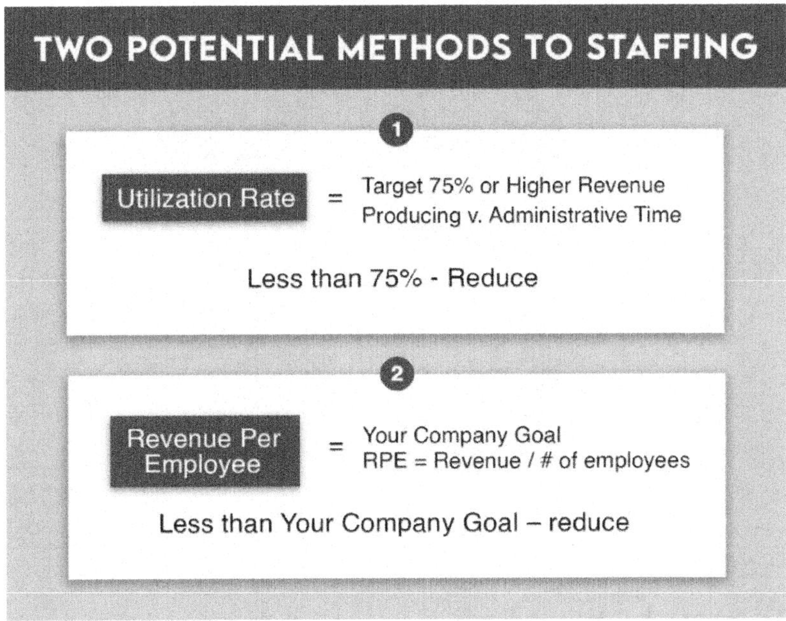

Wasteful Spending

Similarly, consider eliminating waste of resources from your business. Place stricter limits on the use of office supplies and company-sponsored travel. Invest in efficiency by purchasing and installing equipment to make your business more energy efficient. Here is a super-easy way to analyze your spending habits.

Figure 8.5

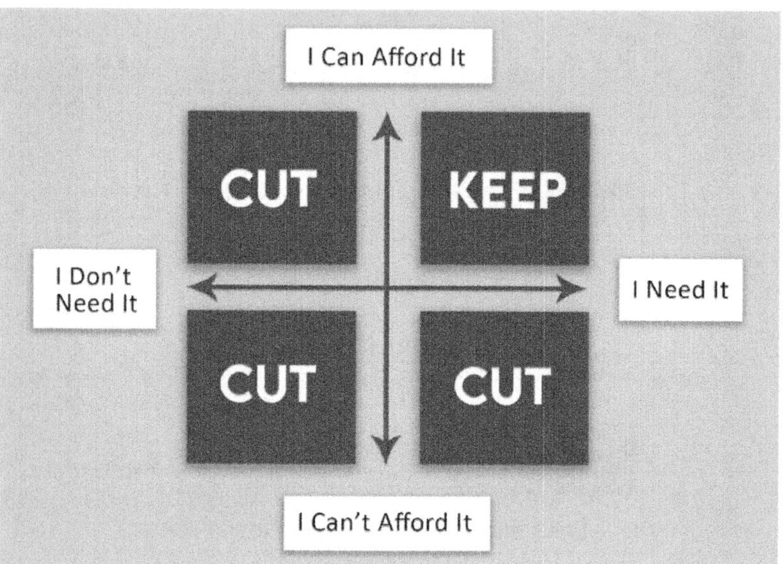

Too much Inventory

Of course, having too much inventory on hand can be a drain on your cash. You spend money with your vendors to keep your goods on a shelf. The more inventory you have, the more money you have sitting on the shelf. This seems pretty basic, but there is another problem that occurs when you have too much inventory.

Producing or purchasing inventory more than what your business needs can lead to a low gross profit margin. How? When you produce too much inventory, you might find yourself having to sell the leftover inventory at a discounted price. Selling on discounted price means low gross profit margin, and low gross profit margin means low net profit. So, you see, how excessive inventory can result in a huge mess and little or no reward for the work you put in.

But we have a treatment available for this problem as well. I know producing extra units can be quite tempting sometimes in anticipation of making more sales. However, after reading the previous chapters, you should agree that managing a Goal Performance Line can save us a lot of hassle. We know that our sample company is not performing well in terms of inventory management. The following are the possible treatments for this problem.

Get Rid of Old Inventory

When you want to adopt a healthy lifestyle, what do you do first of all?

You eliminate all unhealthy foods and habits from your life, and then you follow a healthy routine to make things better. Our businesses work similarly. To maintain a good inventory control system, we first have to get rid of all the trash that is causing chaos. So, to eliminate old inventory, one of the best options is to use the Inventory Master Excel Template on my website to help you analyze each product that you carry. Very quickly you will be able to see the areas where old inventory is occupying precious shelf space. Your goal is to clearance the old or over-stocked items and put your warehouse back into an updated state with fresh inventory. When you're done, take a deep breath and sit back. This is the hardest part of the entire process.

Manage Your Inventory in Real-Time

After you have decluttered your warehouse, the next step is to keep track of your inventory in real-time. Real-time inventory management means recording your sales and purchases immediately through an inventory management software system or any tool that helps you see the movement of inventory through your business. Real-time inventory management optimizes the supply chain, and keeps track of product movement, resulting in overall efficiency in business. In simple terms, using the Items on Hand formula I described above will help you keep more money in the business and the right amount of product on the shelf.

Just in Time Inventory Management

Just in Time, commonly called JIT, is also an effective inventory management system. It is considered as the most effective way to reduce waste in a business. This technique works on a demand-pull basis. Essentially, actual orders dictate the exact quantities of organizations manufacture. It means they make only what is needed when it is needed, and in the amount, it is needed. So, you don't have to keep the unsold stocks taking up your valuable warehouse space. Moreover, less space needed means less storage cost.

Hence, capital expenditure is reduced, and cash can be invested elsewhere. Though JIT is an effective way to reduce storage, it doesn't work well with all types of businesses. Especially if the production time is long and your customers expect quick delivery. As the same medical treatment doesn't work on all the patients, similarly, the same techniques are not necessarily helpful for all businesses. So, the key is to choose a method that best suited according to the needs of your business. The bottom line is to understand how much product your company needs on a regular basis. If you sell 10 units of a product a month and can get a weekly delivery; you might only need 3-4 units on the shelf at a time. This is how you use the Items on Hand formula.

Low Sales Volume

The sales volume of our sample company is way lower than the average sales volume in the industry. According to the root cause map, we identified that the Sample Company is aggressive when it comes to collecting on invoices to their customers. Though it's a good thing to be quick in collections, aggressive collections can make you lose your sales. I always say try to stay close to the industry average. If you do, you know you're meeting your customers' expectations, and you can speed up collections on a short term basis if you get into a cash flow problem. When you don't allow flexible credit terms to your buyers, they may choose another vendor and cause you to lose your sales. Therefore, your company should have a sales manager that knows how to develop an effective collection strategy that is neither too flexible nor too aggressive. So, the first solution to this problem is to hire a new sales manager. He can be aware of the problems that happen in the marketplace and make his job more difficult to perform.

Here is something cool we noticed about this company. They have the capacity to grow. Their competitors all produce more dollars in the Sales to Assets ratio then they do. This means that with the same amount of equipment, our sample company could sell more goods without making an additional investment in equipment. This is important to know because you don't want to start a sales push and not be able to keep up with customer orders.

Knowing who your product is for can be the key to increasing sales. Oftentimes, businesses are too focused on creating and improving their products that they don't realize the importance of setting a specific target audience. Your target audience must be clearly defined. You can't sell your product to everyone. There is a specific group of people who can be interested in buying your product, and you must know that. When you know about your potential customers, you can market your product well. Similarly, creating a competitive advantage is important to stand out in front of your competitors. If a product is already available in the market, why would a potential buyer want to buy from you? What differentiates your products from the ones already available in the market?

Remember you can't chase money in the marketplace. You have to attract it.

By identifying your value proposition (your promise to the customer) and your competitive advantage (why they should buy from you), you can experience that "hockey stick" growth curve that all successful companies have.

Moreover, learning and executing effective negotiation techniques is also significant. Skilled negotiators are usually quite concerned about finding a solution or an arrangement that is satisfactory to both parties. They look for what are called "win-win" situations, where both parties are happy with the results of the negotiation. One of the things you might negotiate is the terms of the sale with your customers. It means you offer better or flexible credit terms to earn your customer's business. This is risky, but it is one of the best ways to build a solid and long-term customer base. Similarly, expanding your product line can benefit you in the long run because some customers want a one-stop solution to all their needs. When you offer more products and options, the chances of improved sales enhance.

Mis-Financed Assets

One of the problems we identified was that this company had mis-financed some of the assets it bought when it expanded its operation. In other words, they used short-term loans to finance some of its long-term equipment assets. Mis-financing is the silent killer of businesses because it sucks cash out of the business in the form of interest payments.

In the Home Run Financial System, I explained that short-term debts are always more expensive than long term loans. You pay more interest on these loans. More interest means more cash outflow, higher interest expense, and low net profit. So, the best method to solve this problem is re-finance plant expansion with a long-term loan. This means you must get the bank involved. If you have used a credit card or line of credit to buy an asset that you can depreciate, see a banker and have them help you re-finance the loan today.

Here is the rule to remember when buying assets for your business:

The length of the loan should match the life of the asset.

This means that if you can depreciate the asset for 5-7 years, you should finance the purchase with a 5-7-year term loan. Pretty simple rule to follow right?

All the above methods will work only when you are consistent. Treatment or therapy always takes some time before you see its effects. So, if you expect overnight results, you might end up disappointed. Develop a plan and work the plan. Good things always take time. If you really want your business to perform better than your Goal Performance Line, patience and consistency are the keys. In no time at all, you will put those hidden cash opportunities in your bank account.

Chapter 9
THE FAST MONEY FORMULA

So, how did it feel being a financial doctor of your or your client's business?

Quite eye-opening it was. Wasn't it?

You have now become almost an expert in not only identifying the problems of business, but you have a method of solving them as well. So, let's answer another very important question i.e. how to attract cash to a business. Flashback to chapter number 1, where we discussed how to start with an end in your mind. We talked about different examples where we analyzed how much money we or our clients will need at a certain point in the future to fulfill their goals.

The transferable value number now comes to life, because now we will look at some of the ways you can put more cash away for your dream. Let's take an example of a new business that just entered the market about a year ago and is doing pretty well. It is a manufacturing company and its hot-new product is selling out fast. Customers love its product and the business is getting reorders quickly. In short, the company is growing month over month. Sounds interesting right? Everything seems so perfect. However, you will be amazed to know that even successful companies can run out of money. Every year, approximately 50,000 businesses file bankruptcy, but it's estimated that 35 percent of them show a net profit on the income statement. They're making money and still filing for bankruptcy. What's going on here? This scenario plays itself out time and time again. Even the corporate giants fall victim to cash flow problems. When you don't understand the components that drive cash through your business, a profitable business can have problems paying its bills.

Here are the top ten reasons why most businesses fail.

1. Lack of experience
2. Insufficient capital (money)
3. Poor location
4. Poor inventory management
5. Over-investment in fixed assets
6. Poor credit arrangements

7. Personal use of business funds
8. Unexpected growth
9. Competition
10. Low sales

If you read these reasons carefully, you will realize that seven out of ten problems indicate a poor cash flow management. I bolded them to point them out to you. Now the question arises, what are the causes of poor cash flow.

According to my experience, here are the primary reasons for poor cash flow. Of course, you can come up with some other causes as well based on your own experience.

1. Focusing on profit instead of cash flow
2. Ignoring the relationship between receivables and payables
3. Paying suppliers too quickly
4. Carrying too much inventory
5. Bad invoicing practices
6. Extending credit to the wrong customers

Successful business owners become obsessed with generating gross profit, but you also have to connect it to cash in the bank. Gross profit is just a figure on paper. Businesses don't run efficiently based on a written profit amount. They need real cash to operate. Imagine that your or your client's business is earning way more than the industry average in terms of gross profit, but your customers aren't paying you on time. You might even find that your bad debts are increasing. Would you have enough cash to stay open in that case?

Obviously, you will run out of money at some point in time. Nevertheless, nothing to worry about because Cashflow Mike is again here to help you out. In this chapter, we will discuss everything that can help us control the speed of our cash flow. Yes, you read it right. We always measure the speed of light, vehicles, or any other object in hours, kilometers, and so forth. Today, we are discussing ways to control the speed of our cash. It is really important to make your business operate efficiently.

Therefore, I created The Fast Money Formula.

Put Your Company in Gear

Your business is begging to be the most efficient

machine it can be. It only feels right behind the wheel when it is purring down the highway. However, a struggling business feels like a machine that's out of sync. It's the decisions the management makes that keep it from reaching its full potential.

A well-run business acts like a machine, where cash is both the fuel and the output. The goal is to create a self-sufficient machine where the business can produce its own fuel. Let's look at a few of the initial indicators that tell managers their business needs a tune-up.

So, as our business is a machine, you have to have a process. Here are the 6 Steps in The Fast Money Formula.

1. Calculate the key ratios of the cash conversion cycle.
2. Calculate the Cash Gap in your business operation.
3. Calculate how much money your company has access to.
4. Calculate how much money your company needs to operate.
5. Determine if your company has a surplus or deficit.

6. Identify any areas of improvement in your cash conversion cycle.

Looks confusing? Let's elaborate on it.

Step 1 – Calculate the key ratios of the cash conversion cycle

Cash Conversion Cycle

Money moves in a very particular way through a company. There is usually a cash outlay that your company makes before cash comes back to you in the form of collections. Although there is a difference between inventory-based companies and service companies, the core principles still apply. In this first step, you will want to revisit the calculations you did in Chapter 6 – ANALYZE. Specifically, you will need to use the following results.

1. Inventory Days
2. Accounts Receivable Days
3. Accounts Payable Days

Below is a copy of those results. We are going to need the numbers in the circles to calculate the Cash Gap in the next step. So, in this case, our sample company has 90 days' worth of inventory. They collect their invoices in 34 days on average, and they pay their bills in 56 days.

Figure 9.1

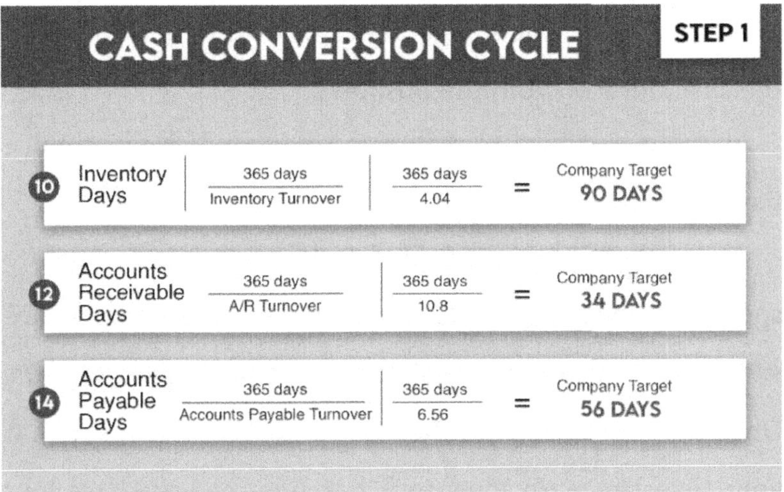

So now what? Well, before we dive into the deep end of the financial pool, let me explain the cash conversion cycle in action.

Cash Outflow

To start the cycle, a company will order some inventory. That inventory will sit on a shelf for a specific number of days. During that time, the invoice for the inventory sits on the company's desk for a specific amount of days. Now events tend to happen simultaneously. The company will sell the inventory, and they will also pay the invoice from the vendor.

What I've described is a series of events that make up the cash outflow from the business.

Cash Inflow

Once the inventory is sold, if cash is not collected on the spot, an invoice is given to the customer. Then this invoice sits on your customer's desk for a specific amount of days. Once the customer pays the invoice, you can now say that your investment in inventory has now returned to your bank account. The cycle is money leaves to purchase the asset, then returns when you trade the asset to a customer for cash. Here is a diagram to help visualize this interaction.

Figure 9.2

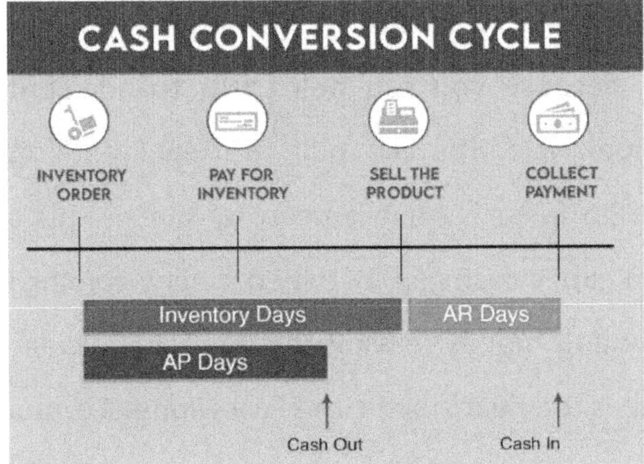

Now let's overlay the cash conversion ratios to put the timeline of events into perspective.

Figure 9.3

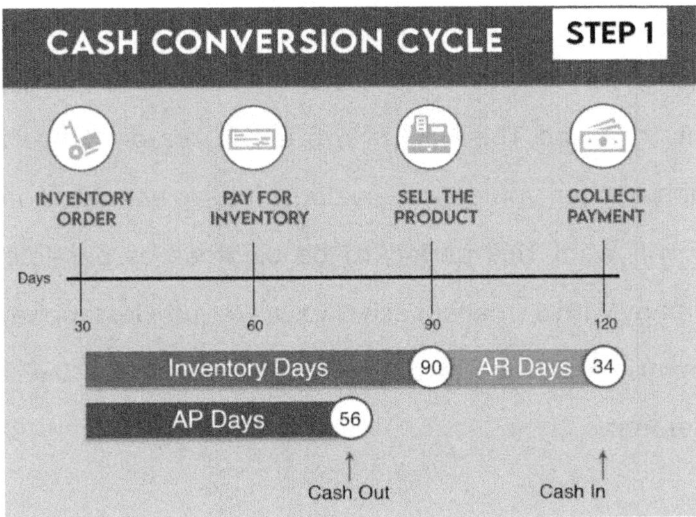

I think you can start to see how cash conversion ratios begin to interact with each other. I like to call these ratios "levers" because you can pull them to adjust the cash conversion cycle. It's like pull the lever and make the machine go faster! What I mean by that is this scenario creates a gap, a cash gap, between money coming into the company and money leaving the coming. Calculating The Cash Gap is the next step in The Fast Money Formula.

Step 2 – Calculate The Cash Gap for your business

The Cash Gap is exactly that, a gap. It is a period of time where your company doesn't have enough money to run efficiently. Because it's a gap, you want to make it as small as possible. Kind of like the Tube System in London, you want to "Mind The Gap". Here is the reason. Since this period is when your company doesn't have enough money, you will want this period to be as small as possible. A company with a smaller Cash Gap will require less money to remain in business. In the next few steps, I'll prove this statement.

Figure 9.4

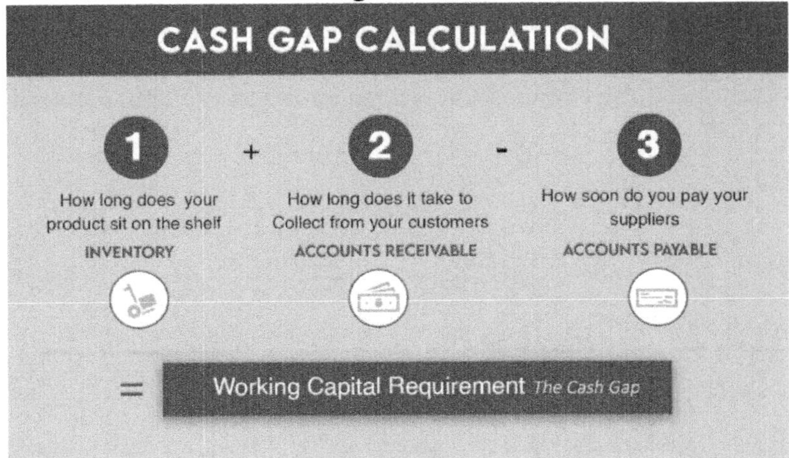

But first, let me explain how to calculate The Cash Gap. It is the period where you have used your cash to pay your bills but are still waiting for your customers to pay your invoices. Here is the calculation.

You add your Inventory Days to your Accounts Receivable Days. This represents the amount of time that you are waiting for cash to come in (CASH IN). Then you subtract your Accounts Payable Days or the amount of time you pay your bills in (CASH OUT). A result is a number of days that represent The Cash Gap.

Figure 9.5

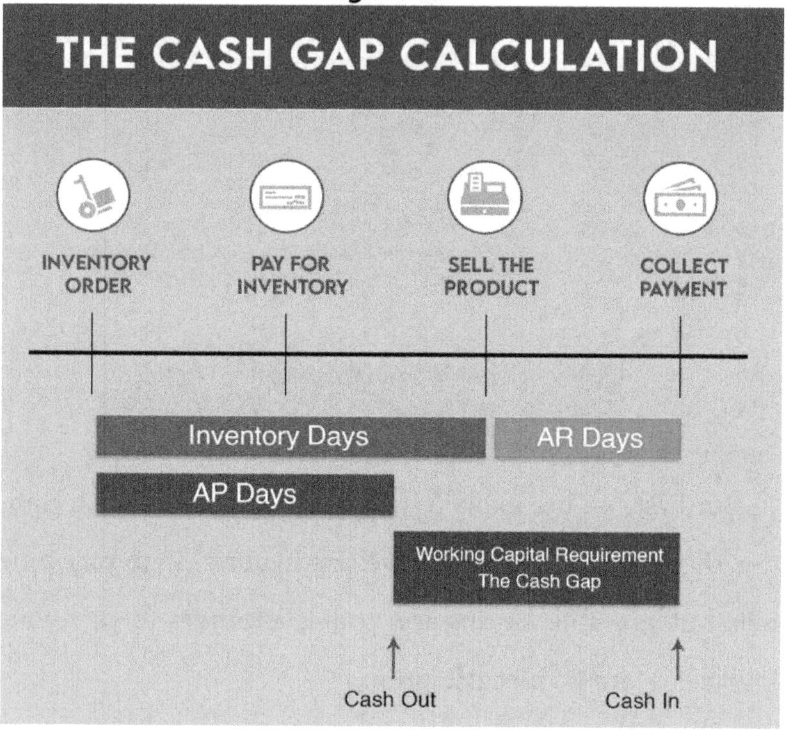

In our sample company, The Cash Gap is 68 Days. The calculation is Cash In minus Cash Out. Also, realize that this calculation is for a company with an inventory. I'll show you the difference in the service company next. See below.

Figure 9.6

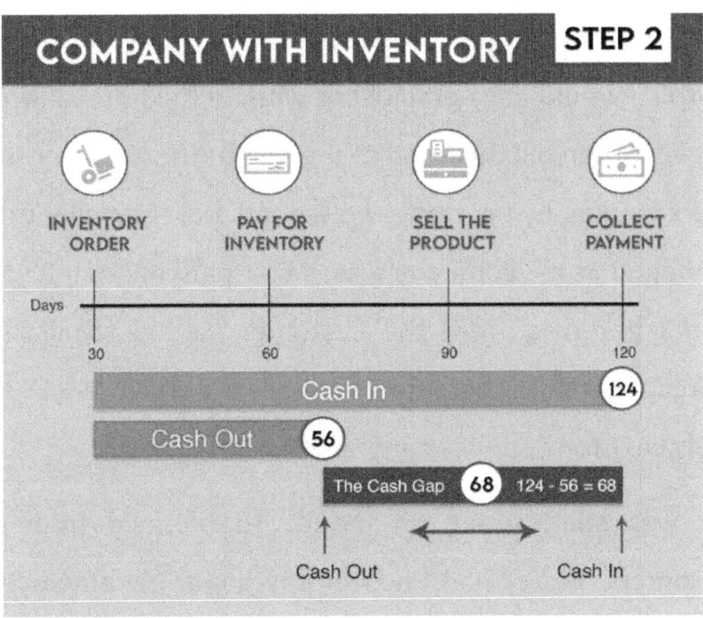

Service Companies

I know what you're saying. "I don't have any inventory" or "I don't have any accounts receivables." It's ok if you don't. Just use zero for those numbers in the above calculation. However, there are services-based companies that don't have any inventory but may have receivables and experience cash flow shortages on occasion. Here is a variation that I used when I owned a hotel staffing company in the Midwest.

First of all, you have to recognize where you have a huge cash outlay in your company. For my company it was payroll. I would have employees work in the hotel all week long and then bill the hotel at the end of the week for total hours worked by my staff. The second and third event that happened in my company was: I first paid my employees, then I got paid from the customer. Sound familiar? It should. I just described the components of the CASH IN and CASH OUT for a service company.

I was still waiting on money to be paid from my customers, while I had to cover payroll for my employees. The combination of these numbers will give you an understanding of how much money your company should have to operate.

Here is the calculation. Accounts receivable days minus payroll period days equals The Cash Gap. Take a look at this example of a company that pays every two weeks.

Figure 9.7

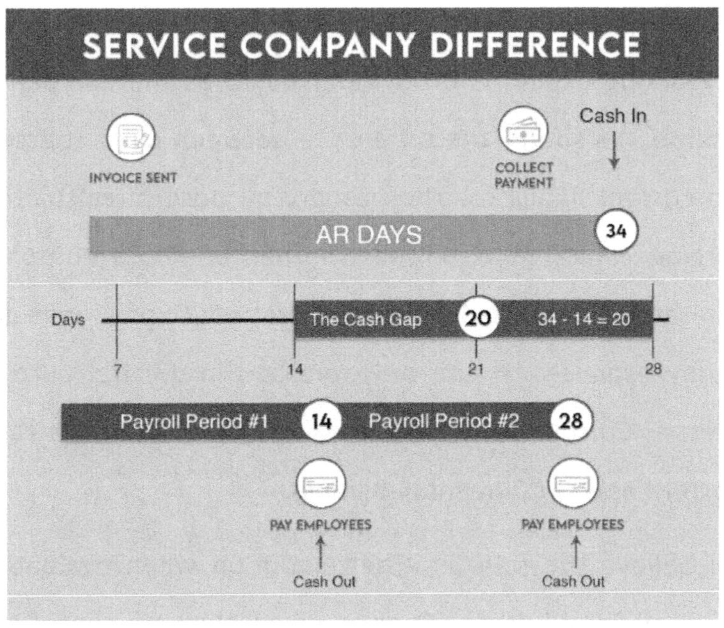

The Cash Gap is 20 Days. So, they will need enough cash or a line of credit to cover 20 days' worth of their operation. Now that we know how much time we need to cover, the next steps will determine how much we have and how much we need in dollars!

Step 3 – Calculate how much money your company Has Working Capital

Working capital is often referred to as the company's cushion. It's simply the difference between current assets and current liabilities. The primary purpose of calculating working capital is to know whether or not a company generates enough cash from its operations to pay for its day to day expenses. It can be expressed in dollars (Current assets – Current liabilities) or it can be stated as a ratio (Current assets / Current liabilities).

I believe the ratio is a better option when evaluating your company because it gives you a clear picture of the company's performance. But, to calculate the amount of money we need in our company, we must translate everything into dollars. So, below is the sample company data to understand their working capital position better.

Figure 9.8

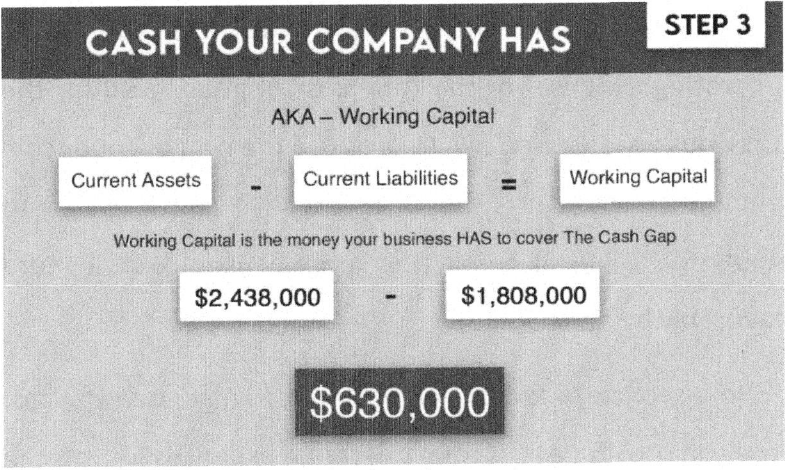

This calculation works the same for all companies and helps us determine how much money is available to cover the obligation that we have during The Cash Gap. What is doesn't tell us is if we have enough. We know we have $630,000 available, but how much do we need. Step 4 is the calculation of how much your company will need to have access to run efficiently.

Step 4 – Calculate how much your company NEEDS Working Capital Requirement

Now the question arises, how much cash you need to close this gap? There are a couple of schools of thought on how to calculate the amount that a company will need. In inventory-based companies, you can use their total operating expense, or the total cost of goods sold for the previous year. Personally, I like to use the cost of goods sold amount because it is most conservative and if I need to apply for a line of credit, this amount is looked at more favorably by bankers.

In a service-based company, you also have two choices. You can use 45 days of total operating expenses, or you can use the total annual payroll amount for the company. Again, I have a preference. I like to use the total annual payroll amount because it is an exact number that matches closely to my calculation of The Cash Gap Days for a service company. In such a situation the following formula comes for our rescue. It helps us know how much working capital is required to finance day to day operations.

Whether it is a company with inventory or a service company we have to convert the number we choose into a daily amount. That way we can apply the daily amount to the number of days in our Cash Gap.

For a company with inventory, I am going to use the cost of goods sold amount from the sample financial statements. That amount is $5,855,000.

In my service company example, I am going to use $2,600,000 as the total annual payroll expense amount for the prior year.

In the calculations below, you will see that I first covert the expense amounts into a daily expense. Then I multiply the daily expense by The Cash Gap Days to determine the company's Cash Need. Below are the calculations for both types of companies.

Figure 9.9

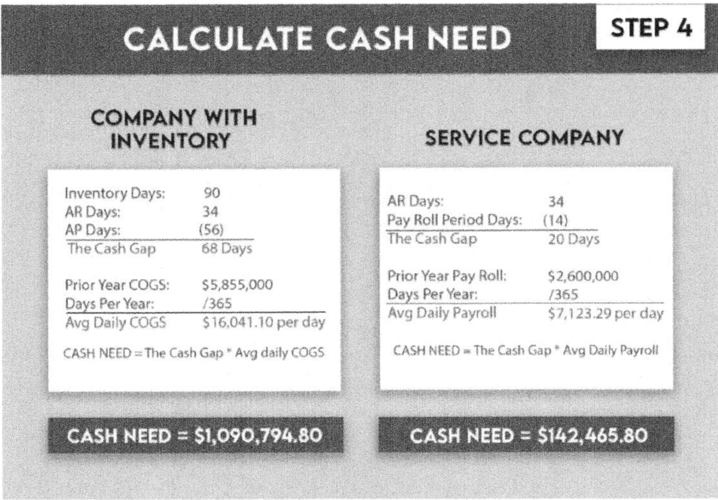

In each case, we can now see how much money the company needs. The company that is holding inventory has a working capital need of over $1,000,000, while the service company only needs to have $142,000. Do we have enough? We have all the information, so let's move to the next step and see if we have enough money or do, we need more?

Step 5 – Calculate if your company has a cash surplus or deficit

We now know what our company needs to operate and what we have. Now just compare the two. This is probably the easiest part. Just subtract what you have from what you need. The results are shown in the figure below.

Figure 9.10

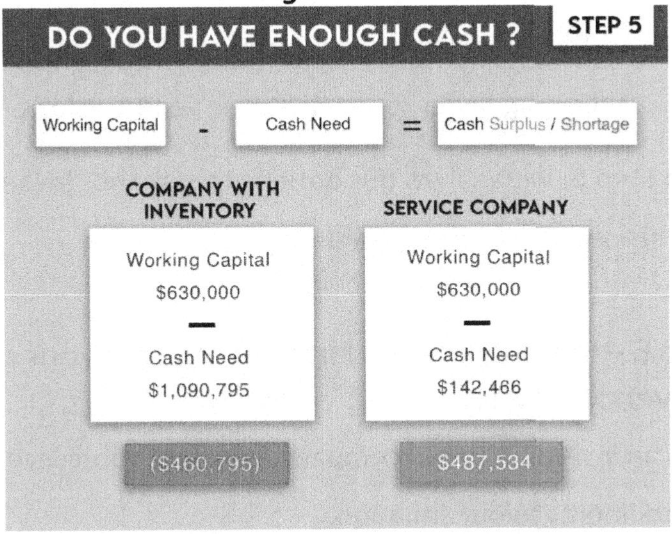

DO YOU HAVE ENOUGH CASH ?
STEP 5
Working Capital - Cash Need = Cash Surplus / Shortage
COMPANY WITH INVENTORY
Working Capital
$630,000
—
Cash Need
$1,090,795
($460,795)
SERVICE COMPANY
Working Capital
$630,000
—
Cash Need
$142,466
$487,534

The results are clear. Our sample company needs an additional $460,795 to run efficiently. While our example service company has plenty of money to operate.

When you see this result, you start to have choices. Obviously, the company with inventory will need to make some changes in the way it operates. Here are two courses of action they could take.

1. Bring in an additional $500k through capital investment or secure a short-term line of credit.

2. Make their Cash Gap smaller by pulling the "levers" of the cash conversion cycle - reducing inventory, collecting faster, or paying their vendors slower.

In Step 6, we analyze our options to pull the "levers" in our business to shrink our Cash Gap.

Step 6 – Identify areas of improvement in our cash conversion cycle

In an inventory based company, you have three levers to pull to improve your situation.

1. **Reduce the amount of inventory you carry-** In our sample company, this might be a good route since we already identified that they have more than the industry average. Based on our analysis in Chapter 7 – DIAGNOSE, we determined that they had an additional $383,000 in inventory compared to their competitors, or an extra 30 days' worth. The industry average is 66 days.

2. **Collect from your customers sooner**- Chances are this option isn't viable. We already collect pretty fast at 34 days when the rest of the industry collects in 44. I'd hate to

recommend collecting faster from our customers for fear of chasing them off. In this case, I wouldn't make a change.

3. **Pay our vendors slower-** I'd say the same thing here as I did for our accounts receivable. I wouldn't risk paying slower when everyone else pays their vendors in 34 days. It could hurt our relationship or pricing with the vendor.

With this in mind, it looks like our best chance as shrinking the Cash Gap is to reduce inventory. In the calculation below, I reduced the amount of inventory we carry to 60 days' worth. It's around the industry average and a round number for easier math. Reducing inventory will reduce the gap. See below.

Figure 9.11

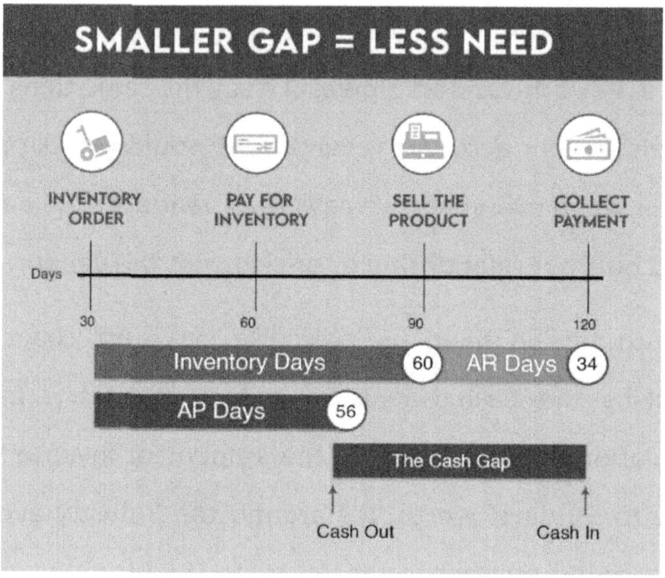

See the gap has shrunk. Now let's calculate the difference in dollars needed to cover our operation. This is where the proof is.

Figure 9.12

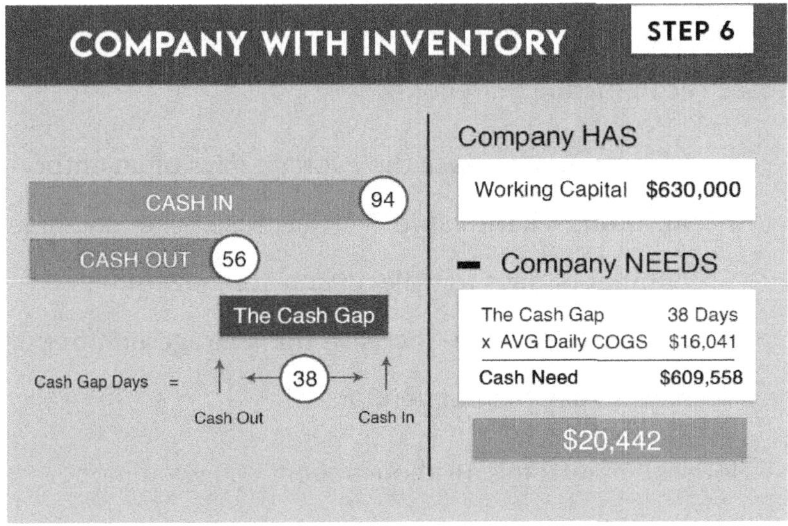

Look at that! By changing the amount of inventory, we carry, we not only put more cash into the company, but we now have a Cash Gap surplus. There is no need to infuse the company with capital in the form of owner contribution or a line of credit. Just run your inventory down through attrition!

I hope you understand that you need your company's cash gap to be small. This means to manage to the fewest amount of gap days possible.

Here is a reminder. To control the size of The Cash Gap, you have the following three levers that should be pulled in these recommended directions.

1. **Inventory-** Decrease the average days of inventory
2. **Accounts Receivable** - Decrease the average number of days to collect from your customers
3. **Accounts Payable-** Increase the average number of days to pay to your vendors

Here the point.z It is all about speed. You want money to move through the company as fast as possible, where money coming in and money going out is at relatively the same pace. The perfect situation would be to match your income and expenses to the same day, and always have a little (read a lot) left over to distribute to owners or invest in growth. That is not always possible, but a guy can dream, can't he?

Chapter 10
FORECASTING BY THE NUMBERS - A STEP BY STEP GUIDE

Every business needs direction. "Where are we going?" is the first question that we should ask ourselves as business owners. Unfortunately, this is the question that most business owners skip because they don't understand the value of forecasting future for a business. I have come across many business owners who skip this significant step just because they think "who can predict the future?"

Astounding, isn't it?

Yes, I agree no one knows what is going to happen in the future. Even so, we can't become indifferent. If this were the case, why would meteorologists' issue daily forecasts regarding weather? Why would they issue alerts to warn the public about anticipated thunderstorms or tornados? I'm sure there are many times the weatherman feels the same way. Yes, many times, weather predictions go wrong as well, but the main purpose of these forecasts is to be aware of the possible dangers so that the precautionary measures can be taken. The same is the case with businesses. Forecasting is necessary so that businesses can develop plans and strategies ahead of time to avoid or cope with any problems.

Let me share an amazing quote by David H. Sandler with you. He said,

"If you want to know what the future holds, you have to bring it into the present."

The quote is powerful on many levels. While Sandler was referring to understanding the buying process of a customer during a sale, I believe this quote is relevant to almost anything you are uncertain of. Whether it's your business or your client's, the future of the business is always unknown. And to make things work smoothly, you always need something that can guide you through. The good news is the guideline is right there for you. I have prepared a five-step forecasting guideline that will help clear the fog of uncertainty away from your or your client's mind. It is a step-by-step approach to looking at a business through the eyes of the financials and bringing the future into the present on paper. Check out the website for a FREE Excel Template to use with this chapter. www.cashflowmike.com

I see a lot of businessmen who forecast the future of their business by trying to create a projected income statement with expected profit. It's a great start but it doesn't help with managing cash. You already learned in the previous chapter that earning profit and managing cash aren't the same things. The best thing about this five-step guide is it goes well beyond just forecasting the income statement. It includes techniques to forecast the balance sheet and determine a safe growth rate for your or your client's business.

The 5 Steps of Forecasting

1. Build transferrable value
2. Create a Pro-forma income statement
3. Build a cash budget
4. Forecast the balance sheet
5. Calculate sustainable growth rates

Build Transferable Value: Start with the End in Mind

Since we are on the tenth chapter of this book, Transferable Value must not be an unfamiliar term for you. This was the first thing we discussed when we started our book. Remember, "start with the end in mind." Since we have already discussed a lot about starting with the end in mind, we are moving to the next step. If you want to take a quick overview of the transferable value, just skim through chapter number 1.

Create a Pro-forma Income Statement: Watch the Business in Action

From the first chapter, we got the transferable value amounted to $91,654.99. To keep it simple, we rounded it off to $92,000. Since now you have laid the groundwork for a long-term relationship with your client, you can now focus more specifically on the one-year financial plan. The first step in this process is forecasting the income statement.

Conventional forecasting methods normally start with looking at last year's sales performance and creating a new forecast with anticipated growth or changes in expenses. They ignore the transferrable value contribution we calculated above. This is one of the ways you can be different as an advisor. Don't leave your client's dream to chance. Create a high-level Pro-forma income statement to see if it can be done.

We will start working by taking the actual year income statement of a sample company. Then we will use the data from it to make our forecast for the next year.

The steps to create a forecast are

Figure 10.1

INCOME STATEMENT COMPANY

Elevate Financial Training

Fill in the amounts in Yellow boxes

INCOME FORECAST	Actual Year 5 In (000's)	% Of Sales	Projected Year 6 In (000's)
Total Revenue	$8,449	100.0%	$12,800
Cost Of Sales	$5,855	69.3 %	$8,732
Gross Profit	[illegible]	30.7 %	[illegible]
Operating Expenses	$2,210		$2,438
Non-Cash Operating Expenses	$218		$181
Total Operating Expenses	$2,427	28.7 %	$3,619
Total Operating Income	$167		$249
Other Income (Expenses)	$(154)		$(148)
Net Income Before Tax	$13	1.5%	$189
Taxes Paid	$(2)		$(57)
Net Income After Tax	$11		$132

1. Record the actual numbers from the previous year's performance.
2. Calculate a % of sales amount for the Cost of Goods Sold (COGS), gross profit, operating expenses, and net profit before taxes. This step is also called Common Size Analysis or Vertical Analysis.
3. As you can see in the above statement that the performance of our sample company is quite poor in the actual year. It earned a net profit of only 0.15% of sales. For the next year, I projected the net profit to be 1.5%, or closer to the industry average.
4. Start with a net profit after tax amount that includes the transferrable value contribution from above ($92,000) and money to leave in the business. I chose $132,000.
5. Then I'll estimate a 30% income tax rate and enter $57,000 as my tax payment. This might be a high estimate, but it provides a more conservative result.
6. Interest will be down to $148,000 from $154,000, according to our loan amortization table.

7. Add interest to net profit before tax to calculate the operating profit amount.
8. To increase your net profit expectation, you can reduce the operating expense % increase. This will also allow you to grow more slowly if you prefer.
9. Record any depreciation from the schedule used for your tax returns. In this case, I chose to use a lower amount of depreciation since we didn't purchase many assets in Year 5. I assumed our depreciation would be reduced in Year 6.
10. The gross profit is calculated by adding operating profit to operating expenses.
11. COGS should be consistent with the previous year's actual percentage of sales unless you anticipate a price adjustment indirect cost.
12. Start with Net Profit After Tax i.e. $132,000. Transferrable value contribution is $92,000. Hence, the profit left in the company is $40,000. Work backward up the Projected Income Statement.
13. The result is how much you must sell to meet your net profit expectation, which includes your

transferrable value contribution. In this case, our sample company will have to sell $12,600,000 in the projected year.

Sprinkle in a Dose to Reality

Although a company's operating expenses are mostly flat during the year, sales rarely are. It is important to understand the sales cycles a business will experience. A good way to visualize this is to create a Monthly Projected Income Statement from the Annual Projected Statement we built in Step 2.

Start by analyzing the historical sales pattern from the last three to five years, if it's available. Break down the sales into a monthly view for each year you have. You should notice that the amounts vary month over month but may fall into a pattern for the same month year over year. For instance, January of Year 1, Year 2, and Year 3 might be similar in their proportional to the annual sales volume. Average the percentage of sales for each month, and use this number to create your monthly sales forecast, as shown on the next page.

Figure 10.2

STEP 2 (A) - BUILD A MONTHLY INCOME AND CASH FLOW FORECAST

Elevate Financial Training

Fill in the amounts in Yellow boxes

INCOME FORECAST	Annual	Jan	Feb	Mar	Apr	May	June	July	Aug	Sep	Oct	Nov	Dec	Total
AVG % of Annual Revenue	100%	3%	3%	4%	5%	8%	17%	25%	15%	7%	5%	4%	4%	100%
Total Revenue	$12,600	$378	$378	$504	$630	$1,008	$2 142	$3,160	$1,89	$882	$630	$504	$504	$12 600
Cost Of Sales	$8,732	$262	$262	$349	$437	$698	$1,484	$2,183	$1,310	$611	$437	$349	$349	$8 732
Gross Profit5	$3,868	$116	$116	$155	$193	$309	$658	$967	$580	$271	$193	$155	$155	$3 868
Operating Expenses	$3,539	$295	$295	$295	$295	$295	$295	$295	$295	$295	$295	$295	$295	$3 539
Non-Cash Ope Expenses	$181	$15	$15	$15	$15	$15	$15	$15	$15	$15	$15	$15	$15	$181
Total Operating Expenses	$3,720	$310	$310	$310	$310	$310	$310	$310	$310	$310	$310	$310	$310	$3 720
Total Operating Income	$148	$(194)	$(194)	$(155)	$(117)	$(1)	$348	$657	$270	$39	$117	$155	$155	$148
Other Income (Expenses)	$(148)	$(12)	$(12)	$(12)	$(12)	$(12)	$(12)	$(12)	$(12)	$(12)	$(12)	$(12)	$(12)	$ (148)
Net Income Before Tax	$(208)	$(208)	$(168)	$(129)	$(13)	$335	$845	$258	$(52)	$(129)	$(188	$168	.	$ -
Taxes Paid	$ 5	$5	$5	$5	$5	$5	$5	$5	$5	$5	$5	$5	$5	$ 57
Net Income After Taxes	$57	$(202)	$(202)	$(163)	$(124)	$(8)	$340	$649	$263	$(47)	$(124)	$(163)	$(163	$ 57

As you can see, the sample company experiences seasonality in their business. Most of their sales are earned during the summer. Knowing this, a business owner can avoid any cash flow surprises and plan to stock up on inventory or labor ahead of the seasonal increase and make downward adjustments in the slower months.

Now let's assume that you and your client believe that the forecast is achievable. So, the next step is to build a cash budget plan to make sure your client can support this type of growth with the funds generated from their business.

1. Build a Cash Budget: You Can't Spend Profit

As I said earlier that creating a projected income statement is a great first step, but it falls short of giving the business owner the critical information they need to make wise decisions. Remember what we discussed in our last chapter. A company that performs very well in terms of sales and gross profit can even run out of cash. To ensure our projected figures are workable, we must create a cash budget based on our Pro-forma monthly income statements. Use your real numbers for accounts receivable and accounts payable. Include your one-time purchases that don't always make it into the Pro-forma such as, new equipment, loan repayments, inventory increases, and so forth.

The cash budget is where the rubber meets the road in business planning. It connects the revenue and expense assumptions a business owner made about the year to the actual way money moves through a company. It's one thing to say, *"I'm going to sell $40,000 in January and spend $30,000 on expenses to make $10,000 in profit."* It's quite another to realize that the $40,000 in sales you made in

January won't hit your bank account until March because your customers typically pay you every 60 days. Additionally, you also have some lag time in how you pay your bills. Even though the expense for an advertising campaign is recorded on your income statement for January, it's possible the invoice for that campaign sat on your desk for 30 days until you made the payment in February.

Here is an example of how you can make assumptions to build a cash budget:

Cash In

Let's say that customers typically pay their invoices in 60 days – (AR Days = 60)

Our budget will start in January, so we need to account for the cash we receive from November and December sales from the previous year. Meaning: November sales are collected in January, December sales are collected in February, and January sales are collected in March.

In our example, we will collect $338k in January and February to get the cash budget started.

Cash Out

Again, let's estimate that our sample company typically pays their invoices within 30 days – (AP Days = 30)

The AP for this example is linked to COGS. We assume that when the client buys inventory, they receive an invoice and pay it within 30 days. The cash-out number will be equal to the COGS number in this cash budget. So, December COGS will be paid in January, January COGS will be paid in February, and February COGS will be paid in March.

In this example, our January Accounts Payable payment will be $176.

Operating expenses will be spread evenly throughout the year. The following cash purchases will be made.

- $30k for a new truck in July.
- $5k for new equipment in January and another $10k for equipment in May.

Now, let's put the two steps together and see the difference between profit and cash.

Figure 10.3

STEP 3 - YOU CAN'T SPEND PROFIT (FORECAST YOUR CASH)

Elevate Financial Training

Fill in the amounts in Yellow boxes

CASH FLOW FORECAST	Jan	Feb	Mar	Apr	May	June	July	Aug	Sep	Oct	Nov	Dec
Cash Balance On Balance Sheet	101	-49	-280	-471	-749	-999	-1375	-2188	-2536	-1003	-31	107
Cash Sales												
Credit Sales	338	338	378	378	504	630	1008	2142	3150	1890	882	630
Other Income (Expense) Net	-12	-12	-12	-12	-12	-12	-12	-12	-12	-12	-12	-12
Total Cash Inflows	427	277	86	-105	-257	-381	-379	-58	602	875	839	725
Accounts Payable	176	262	262	349	437	699	1484	2183	1310	611	437	349
Operating Expense	295	295	295	295	295	295	295	295	295	295	295	295
New Equipment	5				10							
Tax Payment												
Owner Distribution												
Office Remodel												
New Truck							-30					
Total Cash Outflows	476	557	557	644	742	994	1809	2478	1605	906	732	644
Cash Balance	49	280	471	749	999	1375	2188	2536	1003	31	107	81

In the previous step, the monthly income statement showed us that this company will be fine and end the year with $57k. in net profit. However, the cash budget shows a different story. This business doesn't have enough cash to meet its operating needs most of the year. They either need a line of credit or a cash infusion. Otherwise, they will encounter debt collectors until November!

The cash budget is worked vertically month to month, imitating a real-world situation. All January inflows and outflows are calculated before calculating February. The ending balance in January becomes February's beginning balance. See the flow below. The cash beginning balance of $101k comes from the cash amount listed on the balance sheet as of December 31st of the year before this budget, which starts in January.

Figure 10.4

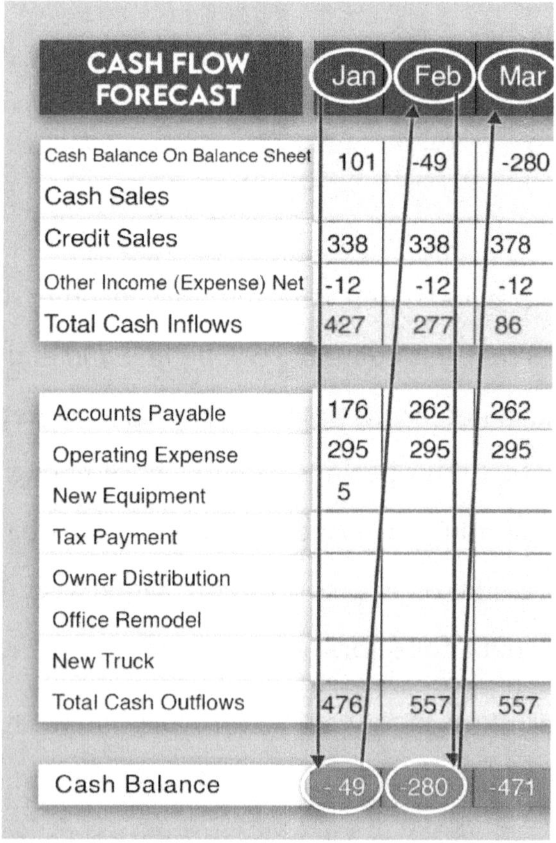

CASH FLOW FORECAST	Jan	Feb	Mar
Cash Balance On Balance Sheet	101	-49	-280
Cash Sales			
Credit Sales	338	338	378
Other Income (Expense) Net	-12	-12	-12
Total Cash Inflows	427	277	86
Accounts Payable	176	262	262
Operating Expense	295	295	295
New Equipment	5		
Tax Payment			
Owner Distribution			
Office Remodel			
New Truck			
Total Cash Outflows	476	557	557
Cash Balance	-49	-280	-471

Notice how the AR collection mirrors the sales from the Monthly Projected Income Statement with a 60-day lag. January sales of $378K are expected to be collected in March. To account for this company paying their invoices, you will see that January's COGS of $262K on the Monthly Income Statement is expected to be paid in February as Accounts Payable. You can start to see the difference between a profit and a cash plan pretty clearly. Using this technique will change the way you operate and put you on a more successful path to getting and keeping cash.

You can also see when you have a cash surplus to make those important purchases for your business. It takes the guesswork out of how much money you have at any given point in time. Adding this step to your planning phase takes the pain out of accrual accounting and helps you properly time your sales to your cash. After all, cash keeps a company alive, not profit.

For the average business owner, this is where the forecasting stops. They tend to be happy with seeing that they can make more money or know when they might run out. However, you can gain a ton of insight by taking one more step and forecasting the Balance Sheet as well.

2. Forecast the Balance Sheet: It Takes Money to Grow

Once the sales forecast has been made, you can also evaluate the items on the balance sheet that have a direct relationship with sales.

Sales cause several things to occur in the business, including increases in accounts receivable, cash and inventory. The more sales we have, the more cash there will be. These are called variable assets because they go up and down with sales. Assets such as land, building, furniture, and fixtures are not directly attached to sales since they take a management decision to increase or decrease.

Sales also cause us to have liabilities. Accounts payable and accrued expenses go up as sales increase; these are called variable liabilities. Notes payable can move with sales, but it is not considered a variable liability.

Instead, when we forecast the balance sheet, we use this account to determine any additional funding the company may need to grow and operate.

It is also expected that an increase in sales will have a corresponding increase in profits.

We, therefore, have the following cause-and-effect relationships. When using the common size forecasting technique, an increase in sales will cause.

1. An increase in variable assets.
2. An increase in variable liabilities.
3. An increase in net profits.

Now, let's assume our sample company grows to $12 million in sales as we projected above. We will also assume they make the 1.5% in net profit. The current balance sheet is shown below in the format used to conduct the forecast. The variable assets and liabilities are calculated as percentages of sales to establish a constant in the forecast.

Figure 10.5

STEP 4 - IT TAKES MONEY TO GROW
(FORECAST THE BALANCE SHEET)

Elevate Financial Training

Fill in the amounts in Yellow boxes

Sales Volume	$8,449,000.00	% of Sales
Net Income	$11,000.00	0.1%

CURRENT YEAR	20X5

ASSETS		% OF SALES	LIABILITIES		% OF SALES
Cash	$101,000.00	1.2%	Short Term Credit	$701,000.00	8.3%
Accounts Receivable	$778,000.00	9.2%	Accounts Payable	$893,000.00	10.6%
Inventory	$448,000.00	17.1 %	Accurals	$214,000.00	2.5 %
Other Current Assets	$111,000.00	1.3%	Other Current Liabilities		0.0%
TOTAL CURRENT ASSETS	$2,438,000.00	28.9%	TOTAL CURRENT LIABILITIES	$1,808,000.00	21.4%
			Long Term Debt	$713,000.00	
Land & Buildings	$1,904,000.00		TOTAL LIABILITIES	$2,521,000.00	
Vehicles	$196,000.00		Owners Equity	$297,000.00	
Equipment & FF&E	$1,316,000.00		Retained Earnings	$1,446,000.00	
Accumulated Depreciation	$(1,590,000.00)		Total Equity	$(1,743,000.00)	
TOTAL ASSETS	$4,264,000.00		Total Liabilities + Equity	$4,264,000.00	
Variable Assets %		28.9%	Variable Liabilities %		21.4%

During the forecast, the client believes they can grow their business from its current volume of $8,449,000 per year to a projected value of $12,600,000 per year. A quick check of the math reveals a growth rate of a whopping 49% (($12,600,000-$8,449,000) / (8,499,000)).

Always check the growth rate % for reasonableness. In smaller high growth rate companies 49% might be reasonable. It's not impossible, but it's still a huge task. By forecasting the balance sheet with this new sales volume, we can see if they have enough cash to grow or if they will need additional investment from the owner or a loan from a bank.

Figure 10.6

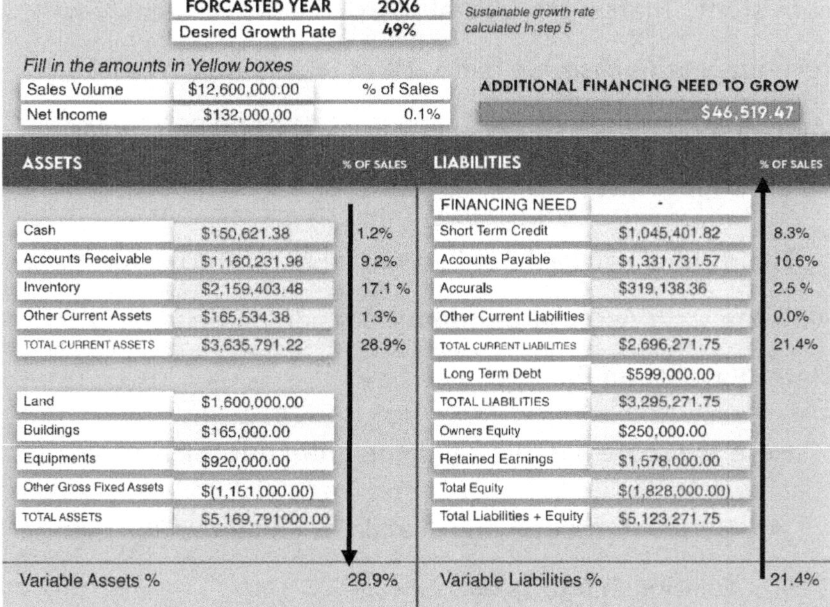

FORCASTED YEAR	20X6
Desired Growth Rate	49%

Sustainable growth rate calculated in step 5

Fill in the amounts in Yellow boxes

Sales Volume	$12,600,000.00	% of Sales
Net Income	$132,000,00	0.1%

ADDITIONAL FINANCING NEED TO GROW $46,519.47

ASSETS		% OF SALES
Cash	$150,621.38	1.2%
Accounts Receivable	$1,160,231.98	9.2%
Inventory	$2,159,403.48	17.1 %
Other Current Assets	$165,534.38	1.3%
TOTAL CURRENT ASSETS	$3,635,791.22	28.9%
Land	$1,600,000.00	
Buildings	$165,000.00	
Equipments	$920,000.00	
Other Gross Fixed Assets	$(1,151,000.00)	
TOTAL ASSETS	$5,169,791000.00	
Variable Assets %		28.9%

LIABILITIES		% OF SALES
FINANCING NEED	-	
Short Term Credit	$1,045,401.82	8.3%
Accounts Payable	$1,331,731.57	10.6%
Accurals	$319,138.36	2.5 %
Other Current Liabilities		0.0%
TOTAL CURRENT LIABILITIES	$2,696,271.75	21.4%
Long Term Debt	$599,000.00	
TOTAL LIABILITIES	$3,295,271.75	
Owners Equity	$250,000.00	
Retained Earnings	$1,578,000.00	
Total Equity	$(1,828,000.00)	
Total Liabilities + Equity	$5,123,271.75	
Variable Liabilities %		21.4%

Currently, our sample company has some short-term bank debt of $701k. They also have a total equity balance of $1,743,000. Using this forecasting technique, these two items are necessary to note. If our sample clients achieve their growth goal, we can expect their balance sheet to look like the figure below. In common sizing, we calculate the variable assets and liabilities to maintain the same proportions to the sales volume of the current balance sheet.

Make sure you keep the variable asset and liability % consistent. Match the actual % to the forecasted % of revenue. In this case, we had 1.2% of $8,449,000 in cash, so we can assume we will have 1.2% of $12,600,000 in cash when we forecast.

Fill in the balance sheet in a U-shaped pattern, starting with the Cash Account on the Assets side and ending with Notes Payable on the Liabilities side.

Here are some notable highlights from our calculations:

- Variable assets and liabilities maintained their relationship to sales.
- To fill in the balance sheet in a U-shaped pattern, you must assume the sheet will balance out. In other words, you must assume total assets will equal total liabilities and equity.
- To calculate equity, you must take the equity balance from the current balance sheet and add the expected net profit/retained earnings from the

forecasted year. In this case, our client should earn $132,000 on $12.6 million in sales as we forecast in the previous step. This increases the retained earnings to $1,578,000 from the current year balance of $1,446,000.

- On the liabilities side, you calculate by subtracting the account values from the total beneath them. For example, to determine total liabilities, you must subtract equity ($1,828,000) from total liabilities and equity ($5,123,271.75).
- Working the liabilities side backward leaves Notes Payable as a variable we can use to balance the sheet. In this case, we can see it will not balance with a value of $0. So, we add a Financing Need Column to make the balance sheet balance.

It's interesting. Isn't it? But there is a thing I am sure most of you have missed. If you carefully look at the image above, you will see that total current liabilities are equal to $2,696,271.75. Since these are the variable liabilities, these accounts are what we will use to make sure the balance sheet balances.

However, if we add up the total liabilities and equity, we get a total of $5,123,271.75. It is $46,519.47 short of balancing with the asset side of the balance sheet of $5,169,791.22. So, is this a miscalculation?

No, this is something I wanted you to think over. The last part of this forecast is balancing the balance sheet. In order to sell $12,600,000, this company will require an additional $46,519.47 in investments or loans (Financing Need $46,519.47 + Short Term Credit $1,045,401.82 + Accounts Payable $1,331,731.57 + Accruals $319,138.36 = Total Current Liabilities $2,742,791.22). You can see the Financing Need calculated in the image above.

Otherwise, they run the risk of "growing broke," or not having enough money to maintain your operation while you are expanding your business. That's right: It is possible to grow too fast.

Here is what the forecasted balance sheet looks like after we add in the additional financing.

Figure 10.7

FORCASTED YEAR	20X6
Desired Growth Rate	49%

Sustainable growth rate calculated in step 5

Fill in the amounts in Yellow boxes

Sales Volume	$12,600,000.00	% of Sales
Net Income	$132,000,00	0.1%

ADDITIONAL FINANCING NEED TO GROW: $0.00

ASSETS		% OF SALES	LIABILITIES		% OF SALES
			FINANCING NEED	$46,519.47	
Cash	$150,621.38	1.2%	Short Term Credit	$1,045,401.82	8.3%
Accounts Receivable	$1,160,231.98	9.2%	Accounts Payable	$1,331,731.57	10.6%
Inventory	$2,159,403.48	17.1 %	Accurals	$319,138.36	2.5 %
Other Current Assets	$165,534.38	1.3%	Other Current Liabilities		0.0%
TOTAL CURRENT ASSETS	$3,635,791.22	28.9%	TOTAL CURRENT LIABILITIES	$2,742,791.22	21.4%
			Long Term Debt	$599,000.00	
Land	$1,600,000.00		TOTAL LIABILITIES	$3,341,791.22	
Buildings	$165,000.00		Owners Equity	$250,000.00	
Equipments	$920,000.00		Retained Earnings	$1,578,000.00	
Other Gross Fixed Assets	$(1,151,000.00)		Total Equity	$(1,828,000.00)	
TOTAL ASSETS	$5,169,791.22		Total Liabilities + Equity	$5,123,271.75	
Variable Assets %		28.9%	Variable Liabilities %		21.4%

3. Calculate Sustainable Growth Rates: Growth is a Planned Event

Forecasting, especially if you are expecting growth, can be extremely difficult. We already know that an increase in sales usually requires an increase in both current assets, like AR and inventory, as well as fixed assets, like additional equipment. These increases often lead to shortages in operating cash flow during the growth period, and business owners must rely on bank loans to survive.

So, the question remains: How fast can a company grow without hurting itself or weakening the balance sheet?

The answer lies in determining what the business owner's risk tolerance for debt is. Are they ok with new debt and how much?

Do they want to maintain their current debt to Equity (Total Liabilities / Total Equity) ratio?

Are they willing to accept more risk in taking on more debt?

Once you determine your client's risk tolerance for debt, use the corresponding formula below to calculate the rate of growth they should be trying to achieve.

Here are the variables you will need for each calculation.

- Net Profit Margin %
- Debt-to-equity ratio – Current or Maximum Allowed
- Variable Asset %
- Variable Liabilities %
- Current Sales
- Current Equity

SALES GROWTH % =

$$\frac{(\text{Net Profit Margin\%}) \times \left(1 + \frac{\text{Debt}}{\text{Equity}}\right)}{\left(\frac{\text{Variable Assets}}{\text{Sales}}\right) - \left[(\text{Net Profit Margin\%}) \times \left(1 + \frac{\text{Debt}}{\text{Equity}}\right)\right]}$$

The following formulas will calculate the maximum growth rate your client can reach. To grow further than the results, your client will need to do one or more of these things:

1. Invest more capital – add cash to the business.
2. Find a way to reduce the variable asset % on the balance sheet.
3. Increase the net profit % they earn.
4. Increase the debt-to-equity ratio they are willing to accept.

Sustainable Growth Formula for Maintaining the Same Debt-to-Equity Ratio

This company wants to maintain a debt-to-equity ratio of 1.0. The net profit percentage is 1%, and variable assets as a percentage of sales are 34%.

Figure 10.8

$$\text{Sales Growth \%} = \frac{0.01 \times (1 + 1.00)}{0.34 - [0.01 \times (1 + 1.00)]}$$

$$= \frac{0.01 \times 2.00}{0.34 - (0.01 \times 2.00)}$$

$$= \frac{0.02}{0.34 - 0.02}$$

$$= \frac{0.02}{0.32}$$

$$= 6.25\%$$

This company can grow to a maximum of 6.25% and still maintain a debt-to-equity ratio of 1.0.

Sales Growth Rate for New Debt-to-Equity Target

Let's say the same company decides to increase its tolerance to new debt and raise the debt-to-equity ratio to 1.3 from the current level of 1.0. All other variables are the same as above. The exception is that this formula uses the equity amount on the balance sheet to calculate the new growth rate.

SALES GROWTH % =

$$\frac{\left[\left(\frac{\text{Equity}}{\text{Sales}}\right) \times \left(\frac{\text{New Debt}}{\text{Equity}} - \frac{\text{Old Debt}}{\text{Equity}}\right)\right] + \left[\left(\frac{\text{Net Profit}}{\text{Margin\%}}\right) \times \left(1 + \frac{\text{New Debt}}{\text{Equity}}\right)\right]}{\left(\frac{\text{Variable Assets}}{\text{Sales}}\right) - \left[(\text{Net Profit Margin\%}) \times \left(1 + \frac{\text{Debt}}{\text{Equity}}\right)\right]}$$

By taking on additional capital in the form of more debt, this company can now grow at a maximum rate of 34.55%. Here is proof that growth requires cash.

Sales Growth Rate with No New Debt

Figure 10.9

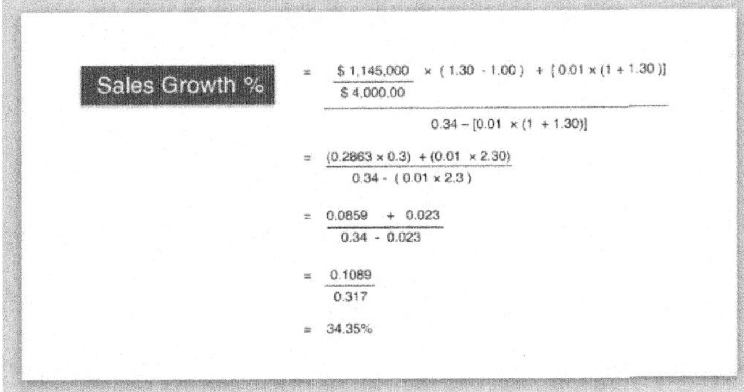

Lastly, here is how much this example company can grow without adding any additional debt to the balance sheet. All other variables will remain the same.

Figure 10.10

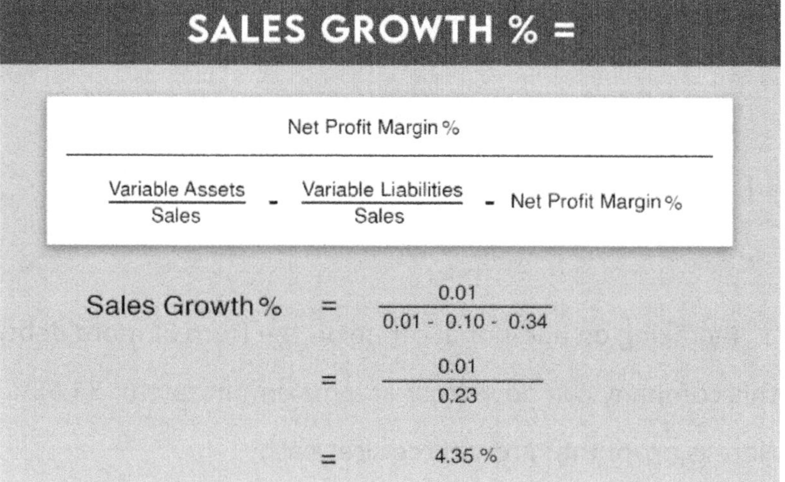

Now the company can experience a modest growth rate of 4.35%.

Forecasting shouldn't be left to chance. It is a very important exercise for any business. Sales performance can vary greatly from month to month. As growth and changes in the business occur, you can act on your role as an advisor by helping your client manage their cash budget and prepare for any anticipated short-term borrowing needs that develop. In our sample company, here are the same three (3) calculations, using the free Excel template found on www.cashflowmike.com.

Figure 10.11

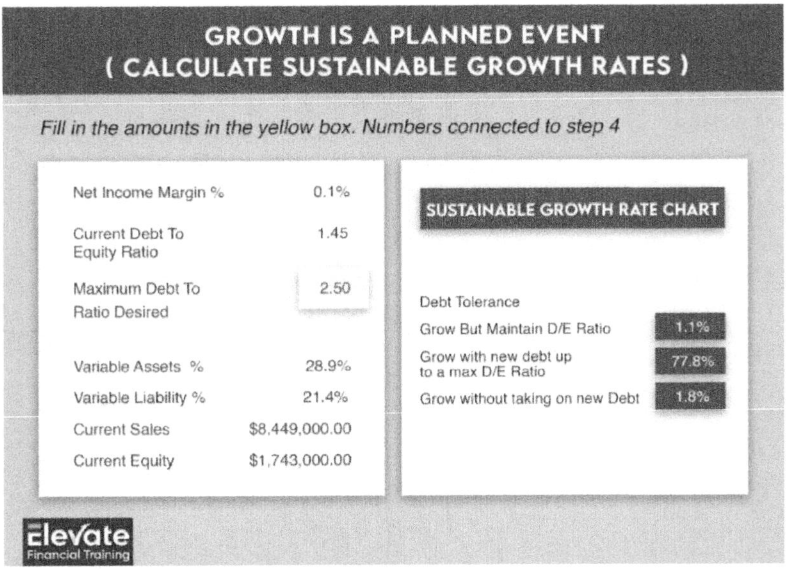

GROWTH IS A PLANNED EVENT
(CALCULATE SUSTAINABLE GROWTH RATES)

Fill in the amounts in the yellow box. Numbers connected to step 4

Net Income Margin %	0.1%
Current Debt To Equity Ratio	1.45
Maximum Debt To Ratio Desired	2.50
Variable Assets %	28.9%
Variable Liability %	21.4%
Current Sales	$8,449,000.00
Current Equity	$1,743,000.00

SUSTAINABLE GROWTH RATE CHART

Debt Tolerance	
Grow But Maintain D/E Ratio	1.1%
Grow with new debt up to a max D/E Ratio	77.8%
Grow without taking on new Debt	1.8%

Elevate Financial Training

For Financial Advisors

As a business advisor, you have life experiences and knowledge that can help your clients. Remember the most likely have one or two businesses that they have to run, while you have worked with 10's, 100's, or more. This step-by-step guide can help them create a foundation to implement your solutions. When you share your life story and experience you impact lives and help them achieve breakthrough moments.

Chapter 11
HOW TO DEAL WITH YOUR BANKER

In his book, *When the Devil Drives,* Christopher Brookmyre, tells an amazing story about modern bankers. He wrote,

"3 people get stranded on a remote Island. A Banker, a Daily Mail reader, and an Asylum seeker. All they have to eat is a box of 10 Mars bars. The Banker says, 'Because of my expertise in asset management, I'll look after our resources.' The other two agree. So, the Banker opens the box, gobbles down 9 of the Mars bars, and hands the last one to the Daily Mail reader. He then says, 'I'd keep an eye on that Asylum seeker, he's after your Mars Bar.'"

What's the point of the story? It portrays a negative image of bankers and the banking industry, doesn't it? Well, it may be true to some extent, but the reality is you can't survive without banks. It is nearly impossible to manage your finances without banks. If you are a business owner, you must be well aware that banks are an indispensable part of your business. There is no shortage of bad things we can say about banks. I mean, after all, they burnt the world down as we know it in 2008. With that in mind, I think about an old Southern saying,

"Stay out of banks. You may never get as rich as you could with other people's money and some luck, but the tradeoff is sleeping at night."

Now, the question is, with all these negative images, how can you develop a healthy and fruitful relationship with your banker? I have a solution to this problem. However, before diving into the details of this solution, let me tell you that most of the time, problems arise due to just not understanding how the banks work. Often, business owners' trouble is that they don't give the banker enough information to work with, or they don't know how their business is being evaluated by the bank. The result is a bad banking experience and a denial of a loan application. Just as a client has complaints with their banker about their services and procedures, bankers also face some issues when dealing with their clients. It is amazing to hear both sides of the story and see that the finger can be pointed in both directions. During the last few years, I have spent a lot of time with small business bankers. The conversation generally turns to examples from our past experiences, both wonderful and horrible. It is during these conversations that I noticed a common theme among the things that annoy the banker. It is interesting because, for over 20 years, I was on the business owner's side of the desk. Not only that, but I was also guilty of getting on their nerves at times. Here are 5 things you can do to frustrate your banker.

1. Show no loyalty to the bank

It is true. Your banker would prefer you to show a high degree of loyalty in your banking relationships. Most business owners don't look at it that way. The typical small business owner has about 15 different bank products that he/she uses in both their personal and professional life. Rarely are they all from the same bank. Just look in your wallet or pocketbook, and you may find a couple of different sources for your credit cards. Then take into consideration your checking and savings accounts, any loans, or investment accounts. Small business owners "diversify" their accounts sometimes on purpose, while sometimes out of necessity. If the truth is told, your banker could handle most of those and strengthen your position and relationship in the bank. However, for a small business owner to do this, they need to have the confidence that the bank is acting in their best interest.

2. Take too much out of the business

Yep, we do. We have other needs for the cash that sits in our small business. Besides, our accountant tells us to do this to reduce our tax exposure. Unfortunately, this issue is where the banker and the accountant are on opposite sides. Both of them have your best interest in mind and it is up to the business owner to balance the two sides of the argument. The accountant wants you to reduce your equity to minimize your taxes. The banker wants you to keep more equity in the company, so he can give you the debt you need to operate and grow the business. You won't always need debt, but if you can forecast out the need in advance, you can adjust your distributions and personal expenses to meet the lending criteria of the bank. If you don't need debt; then, by all means, reduce your tax liability.

3. Wait until it's too late

This is probably the most frustrating part of being a banker. Working with a small business owner who was too far gone by the time they reached out for help. It is a no-win situation for everyone. Most business owners don't understand enough about the cash their business needs to operate and continues to create a huge mound of losses before looking for a solution. At the first sign of trouble, reach out to a banker or accountant for help. You may not like what they have to say, but with your focus, they can help.

4. Unprepared to work with the bank

I have heard hundreds of stories about small business owners that walk into the bank with a box of receipts or a general ledger book, expecting the banker to put together their financial picture. Banks already battle an efficiency problem and are seeking every day to find ways to make our banking tasks faster and simpler. A box of jumbled pieces of paper or a hand-written business ledger is a picture right out of the Great Depression. Not only is this antiquated, but it also makes putting together a loan application in dozens of hours of work. The speed of business has enabled even the smallest of banks and business owners to move with agility and flexibility. There are numerous accounting products on the market, some of them are free, for the small business owner to organize his financials and present a professional package for the bank to evaluate.

Invest in technology that helps you work better with the bank. Then take it a step beyond the organization. Ask your banker to tell you about the key criteria they use to evaluate a loan application. Then use that knowledge to position your company for the best possible probability of your application being funded when you ask.

5. D.U.M.B.

See, it's not just me that thinks this way! This is probably the most common complaint about both bankers and business owners. Imagine both of them pointing the finger at each other, when discussing business. D.U.M.B. doesn't mean that a person is unintelligent. It means the small business owner is good at his trade, but not a financial manager. It's like you are telling the banker "I Don't Understand My Business." They see it in the way you present your financials, can't describe how you make money, have no plan for the future, or operate well below the industry averages. As a small business owner, you have to be the leader of your financial future.

That means understanding the cash drivers within your business and understanding how to best use debt to grow. This is about education. Find ways to learn about the dynamics involved in your financial statements. There is a wealth of experts, articles, videos, seminars, college courses, etc. Take advantage of the information that exists to be the expert society thinks you are. One of the ways to earn their trust is for you to understand the basics of lending. There is nothing more basic than the 5 C's of Credit.

The Five C's of Credit

As a small business owner, if you want to apply for a loan, you have to prove your credibility to the bank. Your banker can't give you a loan just because you own a business. Obviously, your banker gives loans as a way to make money for the bank, but it is a calculated risk that they are willing to take. The following are the five C's of credit that your bank uses to evaluate your loan request. If they like what they see, based on the following factors, they proceed with the deal.

Character

Character refers to your credibility. Your banker needs to be confident that you have the background, education, industry knowledge, and experience required to successfully operate the business. Moreover, your bank may also require a certain amount of management or ownership experience. Similarly, they will make sure that you are a good citizen by making sure you have adhered to the governmental laws and regulations of society. This is the most important factor. If you can't prove yourself trustworthy, your banker will not approve your application, no matter how good the deal may seem to be. I think you would be the same way with loaning out your own money.

Capacity (Cash flow)

While reviewing your application, your banker wants to make sure that your business can repay the loan. The business should have sufficient cash flow to support its business expenses and debts comfortably. Examining the payment history of current loans and expenses is an indicator of your reliability to make loan payments. They are going to look at the financial strength of your company and that includes the ratios we have talked about in previous chapters.

Capital

Your banker will ask how much of your own money you have invested or plan to invest in the business. The debt to equity ratio shows how much skin you have in the game. Obviously, your banker will want to evaluate whether or not you are ready to bear any risk for the business you have requested them to invest in. If you are not willing to take a personal risk for the sake of your business, why would the bank want to?

Collateral

Your banker will consider the value of your business' assets and the personal assets of the guarantors as a secondary source of repayment. Collateral is an important consideration, but its significance varies depending on the type of loan. Your banker will be able to explain the types of collateral needed for your loan.

Conditions

Your banker wants to understand the condition of your business, the industry, and the economy. They will want to make sure if the current conditions of your business will continue, improve, or decline. Moreover, the banker may also want to know how the loan proceeds will be used - working capital, renovations, additional equipment, etc.

The Numbers Behind Your Loan Request

When small business owners apply for loans, most of the time they don't know how much to apply for. However, the case is different for YOU whether you are a business owner or a financial advisor because you are in chapter 11 of this book. You are a financial doctor and you know how to analyze and solve the problems of any company. Just look back at chapter 9 where we discussed the cash gap and the cash flow required to meet the day-to-day expenses of our company. So, if you want to borrow with a short-term loan, just follow the calculations (replace the numbers, of course) given in chapter 9 and it will help you figure out how much short-term debt your company needs.

Similarly, for our long-term debt needs, we discussed EBITDA quite in detail in chapter 2. So have a look back at chapter two and follow the calculation by replacing the numbers. You will get a fair idea about how much is required for your company.

Short Term Loan Amount Calculation – Chapter 9

Long Term Loan Amount Calculation – Chapter 2

Key Figures to Know

1. A Debt to Equity ratio of 2.5 or less is good for a company. This says for every dollar you put into your company, you let the bank invest $2.50 or less.
2. The current ratio should at least be 2 or higher. This means that for every dollar you owe on a credit card, you have $2.00 or more in checking to pay for it.
3. Debt Service Coverage Ratio of 1.25 or higher is good for your company. Meaning, that for every dollar of debt that you have, you have $1.25 or more to pay for it.

How to Apply for a Loan

Do you know what is the key to increasing your chances of getting a loan?

It's the more prepared you are, the better it is.

It is your business, so you are the one who is responsible to educate your banker as much as you can about your business. For this purpose, first of all, you should be well aware of your business and its performance. When you give detailed information to your banker, it helps you increase your creditworthiness in the eyes of your banker. Only 1%

or even fewer customers follow such a detailed process. You can educate your banker about the business by submitting a loan proposal. Your proposal should contain the following items.

Executive Summary- Begin your proposal with a simple and direct cover letter that describes who you are and the terms of your loan request. You want to address things like your business background, the nature of your business, and how the loan will be used to help your company succeed.

Business Description- Write a short description of your business. You will want to include a history of critical events and a summary of your current activity. The banker will want to know more about who you sell to and how you do it.

Management Experience- Describe the expertise that you and your team have in this field. You want to show the banker that you and your team are capable of creating and operating a successful business.

Loan Request- Here you are going to describe the

purpose of the loan, including the amount you are asking for. This is where the calculations I reminded you of above come into play. They show the banker that you understand how your business runs and how money is generated through your operation. You will also want to include how you determined that your requested amount was appropriate. If you have supporting documents like quotes or estimates of costs, include them to support your request.

Loan Repayment- It is always better to start the loan negotiation process with the terms you want. You will want to outline the term of the loan and interest rate. To support your terms, include proof that you can repay the loan. This is where Chapter 10 (Forecasting by The Numbers), helps. Use the Pro Forma Income Statement and Cash Budget to show you projections. Know that they are going to ask you about what happens if you don't meet the projections. If you are applying for a short term loan, like a line of credit, the answer should be that you won't have to borrow as much from your line.

Collateral- If you have something the bank can use as a secondary form of repayment, this is the place to describe it. The bank needs two sources of payment to minimize the risk of the loan. Collateral is something that the bank can sell if your business doesn't make the loan payments with cash generated from your business.

Personal Financial Statements- Include recent financial statements, (within 90 days) for all owners with 20 percent or more interest in the business. A personal financial statement is used to show the bank your net worth. Be prepared to include your tax returns as another form of proof of your financial condition.

Business Financial Statements- This is a no brainer. After all, this whole book was written about these statements. Make sure your income statements, balance sheets, and cash flow statements are up to date. You will want to be prepared to submit these statements for the last 3 years, plus the current year to date.

Equity Investment- An owner must put some of his/her own money into the business to get a loan; the amount depends on the type of loan, purpose, and terms. You show the banker you are doing this by increasing your equity or retained earnings. This is where the bank will check your Debt to Equity ratio. Remember to try and manage this number to 2.5 or less. Some banks will lend when this number is as high as 4.0. However, you want to be in the best position to receive a loan, not just have a small chance.

In addition to these items, there are others that your bank might ask for. They may want to see things like your company's Articles of Incorporation, or contracts that you currently have. Don't worry about it. Just be diligent with their request and provide everything they need on time Remember; they want to find a way to give you a loan.

When your banker knows that you understand everything about your business and you have been clear about your purpose of taking a loan, they love it. Moreover, you have armed them with the best information you can for them to decide to trust you.

How to Develop a Better Relationship with Your Banker

You have to maintain a healthy relationship with your banker even after your loan request is approved. The best banking relationships are based on pro-active communication. Don't be a fair-weather client. Instead, establish a regular pattern of communication with your banker, whether or not you need any help. The following are some of the ways that will surely improve your relationship with your banker.

1. Call your banker at least once a quarter. Share the achievement of your company with them. It will make them feel valued.

2. Most of the time, bankers send holiday or birthday cards to their clients. However, clients rarely reciprocate. Differentiate yourself from others by sending greeting cards to your banker on a birthday or other festivals to make them feel that your care for them.

3. Even if your company is not performing well or your business is going through a tough phase, share this information with your banker before they find it out second hand. Profit and loss are part and parcel of every business. When you share bad news about your business with your banker, it shows to them that you and your business are transparent and credible. Part of earning trust is being able to present your company is a professional manner.

Chapter 12
THE SIMPLE BUSINESS VALUATION FORMULA

As a business owner and advisor, I have come across people from different industries and backgrounds. Most small business owners that I meet are running their businesses successfully. Their businesses generate consistent income streams, and they are happy about it. Sounds great, doesn't it? However, things are not as simple as they seem to be. Your business is not about today only, you have to think in a broader perspective, keeping the future objectives of your business in your mind. I often wonder if generating consistent income streams is enough? It may be satisfactory for many people, but for me, it's just the start.

Creating a small business is not a big deal. It may shock you to hear me say that, but every other day, I hear that someone started their business. From the next Mark Zuckerberg to the next teenager with a lawnmower, they are in business for themselves and initially by themselves. Whenever I read about the increasing number of self-employed individuals, a question pops up in my mind. "Have they started a *business*, or did they just create a job"

Most people don't even realize there is a difference. But there is a huge difference between creating a job for yourself and starting a business. When you create a job for yourself, the income of your business is dependent on you. Once you stop working, the income stops too. However, in actual business, you grow your company in such a way, that it can run and survive smoothly without your daily contributions.

Remember the chapter where we discussed the importance of transferable value? It was all about the value of your business without you in it. According to law, your business is a legal entity that exists independently with rights and liability. Then why should it depend on you? If it's separate it should grow independently.

This is the reason I emphasize starting with the end in mind. Let's suppose when you have earned enough from your business, that you decide that you want to sell your company. Now just think, why would anyone want to buy your business if its continued success is dependent on you? Recall the value drivers of your business that we discussed in chapter 1. The success and effectiveness of your business are represented by two factors:

1. It's the ability to contribute to cash flow

2. It's the ability to continue to generate a positive cash flow under a new ownership

If your business is dependent on you, why would anyone want to buy your "job." Personally, I'm not in the habit of buying your problems. You have to show me the opportunity and reward to get the highest possible value.

Being a business owner, your focus should be on planning and developing your exit strategy from Day 1. Spend your energy finding the right people, who work in the right process, to generate cash for your future.

Challenges You Face When Trying to Sell Your Business

Whether your business is relatively new or old, when you try to sell it, you always encounter a few challenges. This is especially true if you are too much involved in the operations of your business.

Your Employees and Customers

When you treat your business as a job, you create a lot of problems for yourself. Your employees and customers become dependent on you. They see you as the most integral part of the business. As a result, when you plan on selling it, your employees may get nervous and start looking for other options. They are used to working with you and therefore, it is difficult for them to accept this change. You have to remember that people fear loss, not change. They don't want to lose the glue that holds them together every day. In contrast, if you keep yourself focused on developing growth strategies instead of frontline operations, it doesn't make any difference to your employees as to who the owner of the business is. They continue working with the same zeal even if the ownership changes. The same is the case for your customers. When your customers and vendors perceive you and your business as the same entity, they may start to consider switching to your competitors when they know that you are selling your business. Therefore, you must start and grow your business as an owner, more than an operator. You don't want to be seen as a "character in the play."

Value of Your Business

Another problem that most business owners experience while selling their business is, they don't know what they should demand and what offer they should accept. Obviously, buyers will always start making an offer at a very low price. The key to overcoming this challenge is to have a clear understanding ahead of time of the true value of your business and to have the necessary evidence to back that up. Your financial advisor can help you do your business valuation. Once you have a clear understanding of the true value of your business, you can close the deal at the best price.

Dealing with One Potential Buyer at a Time

If you are running your business efficiently, that doesn't mean you can sell it efficiently as well. Many business owners are not interested in hiring a business broker at the time of selling it. It's quite surprising for me because saving that 10 to 20 percent of brokerage amount can cost them a huge loss. Moreover, due to your busy schedule, you can't deal with multiple potential buyers at the same time. Not only does it slow down the entire process, but it also keeps you from getting the best offer. Hiring a business broker is a good option as their network and advertising allow them to quickly and efficiently reach a lot of buyers for your business.

Understanding the Value of Your Business

Understanding the true value of your business provides a realistic outlook from which to plan for the future direction of not only your business but also the future income needs of you and your family. Once the value is known, effective plans and strategies can be put into place for future growth, business continuation, succession planning, and retirement planning. If you are intending to sell your company, knowing its true value is necessary. This process should be started far before the business goes up for sale on the open market because you will have an opportunity to take more time to increase the company's value to achieve a higher selling price. As a business owner, you should know what your company's valuation is. You may have a rough idea of what your business is worth, based upon simple data such as stock market value, total asset value, and company bank account balances. However, there is much more to business valuations than those simple factors.

My suggestion is to complete a valuation of your company on an annual basis. Mainly, because knowing the true value of your company is often a key factor in determining the right time to sell. It also helps to show company income and valuation growth over five or ten years, because you want to understand your growth curve and determine when you have grown the company to the full potential of your ability. Not all of us can manage billion-dollar companies, but there is a sweet spot to your management ability. Selling at the highest level of your ability, physical and financial, is the key to getting the timing of your exit just right.

Now the question is how to value your business. Just like all financial problems, I have a few formulas to help you answer this question as well.

There are about 12 different ways to value your business. Realize this, there is no one-size-fits-all method. All methods work differently depending on the nature of the business. Your financial advisor can help you identify which method is best suited for your company. To help you understand business valuation, the following are some of the ways that you and your financial advisor might consider using.

Asset-Based Valuation

Everything that your business owns has a value and can be shown on your balance as your asset. Assets include land and building, equipment and vehicles, cash, supplies, accounts receivable. Intangible assets like intellectual property also have a value.

Cash Flow

Some buyers want to know how much cash your business can generate. This method uses information from a cash flow statement showing the inflows and outflows of cash for the business over a specific period. This cash flow is then projected into the future under the assumption that $1 today should be worth more in the future. Cash flow value is often used for valuing companies that have shareholders but requires that you can correctly estimate future cash flows.

Gross Sales

Many business owners determine the value of their business based on gross sales over a few years. This may look very catchy, but revenue is the crudest or you can say unrefined approximation of a business's worth. Your sales don't mean that your company is profitable. Therefore, valuing your business based on gross sales is often not a good idea. On the other hand, if someone wants to pay you a multiple of sales, you might listen. It is interesting because most SaaS companies will use this as a valuation estimate.

Multiple of Earnings

This is by far the best method to value a company that has shareholders. The earnings (income or profit) of a business are used to value a business in these multiple methods. In a public company, the earnings multiple is the stock price divided by earnings per share. The resulting figure is also called the Price Earnings Ratio (P/E). But in our small businesses, you can use the Return on Investment (ROI) for companies in your industry as your guide. For example, if the average ROI for a company in your industry is 20%, then the earnings multiple is 5 (100 / 20 = 5). You would then multiply the Free Cash Flow of your company, which is based on EBITDA, by this multiple. The result will give you a valuation.

Since we have talked a lot about cash flows, and gross sales and profit in the previous chapters, in this chapter, I will discuss the two methods that I use a lot to value a business. These are the Asset Valuation Method and Earnings Approach. Based on the data of a sample company, I have applied the two valuation techniques and you will be amazed to see the difference between the results. But understand that I use them to set a value range. The low side is determined by the Asset Approach and the Expected side of the range is determined by the Earnings Approach.

Asset Approach

Ok, as I said, the Asset Approach helps me set the low side of my valuation. This is the number that I think I can liquidate my company for, so I wouldn't accept an offer lower than this number. Why? I can dismantle the company myself and get more. This is why I use this approach to set my negotiation strategy. It helps me identify where I'm willing to negotiate and how much of a discount I'm willing to give. Here is how I calculate it.

Figure 12.1

In the above figure, the book value of the assets of the sample company is $1,743,000. What is the book value? It is assets minus liabilities, or on the balance sheet is it your total equity line. You have to remember that this is just math. If I sell everything I have and pay off my obligations, this is what I should have left. What it doesn't account for is what the future holds for this company. It doesn't look at your current operation, the state of the market and industry, or any other factors that come into play during an actual valuation. So, you have to adjust it. It is the difference between book value and fair market value. You carry your assets on the balance sheet at their original cost minus any depreciation. The truth is this might not be what you can sell them for on the open market. Your buildings, equipment, and land might be worth more. Therefore, the best way to get an adjusted book value is to determine or estimate what your assets are worth on the open market. You can estimate this yourself to get a quick value, or you can have an appraisal of your assets completed.

In our sample company, I estimated that our adjusted book value was $2,743,000, or $1,000,000 over book value for easy math in this exercise. Now comes the fun part. Every potential sale is a planned event, and you need to be prepared to negotiate point by point. If you don't, you could leave tons of money on the table. With that in mind, I set my bottom dollar by lining out the most common negotiate points and determining what my highest discount would be on each item. This amount is often referred to as liquidation discount.

As you see in the above image, I'm willing to discount 20% accounts receivable asset to the new owner, because I know I can sell these open invoices to a factoring company for 80% of the value. Remember, I'm trying to set my bottom dollar by comparing the sales transaction to selling the individual parts on my own.

With inventory, I'm a little more liberal. Mainly because it is a pain the butt to deal with inventory after you no longer have a business. It is worth it to me to sell it at 50% on the dollar to get rid of the headache of moving and storing it. I try to get more at first, but I know that the buyer doesn't have to take any of my inventory. He can just buy all new to start his business.

When we liquidate the company, we will have to sell off the assets. Most of the time, I use a broker, real estate agent, or auctioneer to do this. Yes, there is a cost, so I estimate 10% of the assets to compensate for this cost. I'm willing to discount the price of my assets by 10% to the buyer, so I don't have to go through the selling process with a third party.

Finally, the liquidation process takes time. Therefore, as a way to close the deal, I'm always willing to give the buyer a discount of up to 3 months' worth of operating expenses, so I can avoid the process. Otherwise, I would have to spend that amount of time closing the business on my own.

In our sample company, the total liquidation discount amounted to $1,669,100. When this amount is subtracted from the adjusted book value, we got the bottom-line market value of our company i.e., $1,073,900. The asset-based approach gives you a fair idea about the value of your company based on selling your assets and paying off your liabilities, but it ignores goodwill that is a critical factor. This is the main reason that I use it to set my bottom dollar, I know that my business is worth more than just the value of the assets alone.

For those who are new to valuation, goodwill is basically the intangible value of your customer base and the business you have built. That means the people you have in place, the processes you have developed, the brand equity you have built, all of these helps improve the value of your company. From an accounting standpoint, it is the amount of money that someone is willing to pay over the book value of the listed assets on the business balance sheet. And believe me, you want this number to be a lot!

Now that we know our bottom dallor, we will apply the Earnings Approach to the same company. An asset approach is a historical approach that ignores the market value of your business and the possibility of generating future revenues. But, the earnings approach is based on the idea that the actual value of a business lies in the ability to generate revenue in the future.

Earnings Approach

Figure 12.2

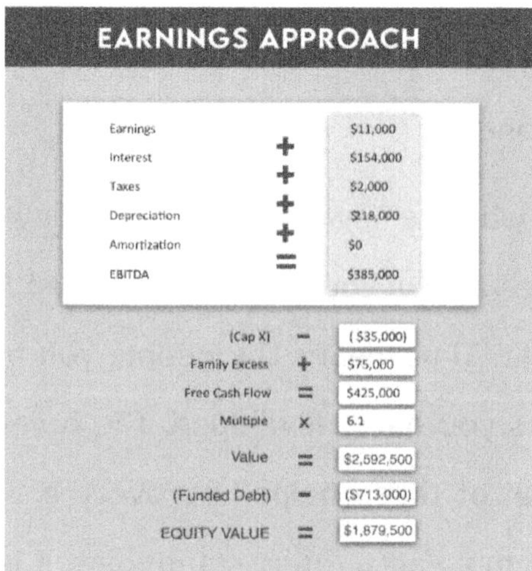

In this approach, we are trying to determine the value of the cash flow that the business generates with its operation. The value this calculates results are more closely related to the fair market value of the company and I use it to set the selling price of the company. It starts with our old friend EBITDA.

To identify the value of our sample company, we calculated EBITDA at $385,000. This amount is then adjusted for Capital Expenditures and Family Excess to arrive at the Free Cash Flow (FCF). In other words, free cash flow (FCF) is the cash left over after a company pays for its operating expenses and maintaining its equipment, also known as CAPEX for capital expenditure. You'll notice that we subtract CAPEX from EBITDA.

This is because we understand that it takes a certain amount of money every year to maintain the equipment, so in this approach, we give the buyer a credit for an amount of money they will need to achieve similar results. Inour sample company, the difference between Gross Fixed Assets in Year 4 and Year 5 was $35,000. This is the amount I estimated was needed to sustain the operation.

Family Excess, also known as, the Owner's Benefit, is added back into the EBITDA amount. First of all, this money represents expenses that the owner runs through the company for their benefit. They are things like vehicles, long term care insurance, country club memberships, etc. In general, these are expenses that the new owner will not have to pay when they buy the business. They will be transferred back to the owner. In our sample company, that amount was $75,000 per year in owners' benefit. By adding this amount back in we now have the company's Free Cash Flow (FCF).

Next, we determine the multiple. It starts with the Return On Investment that the average company in this industry achieves. After all, if the average person gets this rate of return, why can't the buyer of this company? The ROI for the average company was 16.4%. If we divide 100 by 16.4, we can derive a fair multiple for a company in this industry.

The result is 6.1, otherwise said as 6.1x or times.

When we multiply it by the FCF, we get the potential value of $2,592,500. This is the number that I can justify and set an asking price for the company with. But, that isn't the final step. We also have to deduct the long term debt we owe any lenders. Why? Because, once we sell the assets, we have to use the proceeds to pay back out loans. In the Asset Approach, that step is assumed when we calculate book value, assets minus liabilities.

Finally, the amount of debt is deducted to get the net equity value i.e., $1,879,500. This is another moment of truth. When you look at this number, you have to ask yourself if it is enough. Does it fund your transferable value amount we calculated in Chapter 2.? I want this number to be enough to cover the last mile of the journey you walked as a small business owner. It is here that you answer the question.

"Did I build transferable value, or did I build myself a job?" It is the saddest thing in the world to see a seller look at this number and think to himself; "It's not enough. I have to get another JOB." Those are the D.U.M.B. business owners and by now, you're not one of them.

The calculation for both the methods is pretty simple, isn't it? However, the difference is huge. Based on historical data (the value of the company's assets on the balance sheet), you got $1,073,900. Whereas the earnings approach that is based on future projection gave us a higher amount that is $1,879,500. That difference of $805,600 shows you the range that you could expect negotiation to be held between. Understanding the value of your company based on using a multiple of earnings can not only help you determine the best price for your company when you are planning to sell it but can guide you today towards building the value you want when you exit.

Four P's to Supercharge Your Business Value

When you start with the end in your mind, you know where you want your company to go. Based on this information, you can work from the very start to maximize the value of your business. The following are the seven P's that are the drivers to enhance your business value.

1. Product
2. Process

3. People
4. Profits

Product

Nothing happens in your business without having something to provide to your customers. Your goods or services are the main drivers of your cash flow and moving them quickly is the key to improving your value. You will need to have a thorough understanding of the life cycle of your product and your production capability.

- Define your competitive advantage
- Decide on how you establish brand recognition, and satisfy customer needs better than the competition
- Identify your unique resources & strongest asset
- Make sure you are listening to your customers. Too many times, I thought I knew better, and I was wrong.

Process

Processes are important because they describe how things are done and then provide the focus for making them better. Your business process determines how successful the outcomes will be. Therefore, improving or upgrading your organizational structure is important.

- Set your key strategic priorities
- Define tasks employees perform, and how they work toward a single purpose
- Examine all systems such as ordering, delivery, management information systems, accounting, etc.
- Make sure you are taking the shortest route to get things done.
- Remember that franchises are successful because of their scalable and repeatable processes.

People

Another important value driver for your business is People. The people associated with your organization can make or break your business. You need to be sure about what decisions can prove to beneficial for your company when it comes to adding or removing people. You must identify whether or not:

- Make sure you are hiring people who fit into your organization. You can use the "social styles model" to balance out your teams rather than be overloaded with a dominant personality type that is ineffective.
- Focus on each person's strengths to put them in the right role. Many of my conversations today are focused on exploiting the skills that people are great at and they love to do. You get a lot more done in a short amount of time.
- Make quick decisions to move on. If they aren't right for your organization, they become toxic to the rest of the workforce. Be decisive in your terminations to keep the workforce productive.

Profits

Profit is one of the core objectives of doing business. Your potential buyer will also be interested to buy your business if they find it profitable. Optimizing profit margins is the best approach to enhance your business value. You must know

- Understand how the company has profited and where the money is being generated.
- Put controls in place to manage gross profit margin and the operational expenses by practicing Expense Control.
- Run the Financial Doctor Method to find hidden cash in your current operations regularly.

Many business owners think that "I am not planning on selling my business any time soon. So, I don't need to know what it's worth, right now?"

It may seem right, but it's wrong. Understanding the value of your business is not just for knowing how much it will sell for. It is equally essential for the growth of your existing business. No matter which method you use, company valuation is important to a business's growth and overall health. The variables used to calculate your value, are also the same things that put more money in your pocket while you are operating your business. The value of your company if your report card as an owner. It's up to you to put in the work to get an A in small business management.

Chapter 13
THE DELIBERATE EXIT STRATEGY

Whenever a residential or commercial building is constructed, the architects make sure that the building has at least two doors, preferably at the exact opposite ends. So that if any emergency arises and the people inside the building need to leave quickly, there are adequate exits available. Similarly, many constructors build a fire exit separately. In an event, if a fire breaks out, the occupants can immediately evacuate to avoid any possible injury. Now, imagine that you are inside a building that has only one door.

Suddenly, the building catches fire. The place where you are sitting is quite far from the door. How would you feel? Will you panic? The entire situation may leave you so overwhelmed that you become paralyzed by fear. The same thing can happen when you start a business but don’t plan an exit strategy for it. Your business is just like a building where the need for an emergency exit is essential to ensure safety and peace of mind. This is the reason that I always emphasize starting with the end in mind.

Why is an Exit Strategy Important?

By this time, I think you have figured out that we have come full circle. This is the end, I meant when we started this book together. Your departure from your company should be a planned event as much as possible. Because planning gives you options and puts you in the best position to exit on your own terms.

Whenever we talk about an exit strategy, the first thing that comes to our minds is selling our business. Well, that may be the most common way, but an exit strategy isn't limited to just this one course of action. An effective exit strategy is significant for getting you out of day-to-day business operations and focusing on other important areas of your life. What we are talking about is giving you, the business owner a way to reduce or liquidate your stake in a business. If the business is successful, an exit strategy helps the owner make substantial profits. And if the business is not successful, an exit strategy enables the entrepreneur to limit their losses. As a financial advisor, I always advise my clients to start with the end in their minds. When they plan to start a business, they should be clear about where they see it going. Therefore, incorporating a thorough exit strategy into the business plan from the very start can help you set the stage for choosing the best time and structure to support your dream for the future.

I know it may sound a little contradictory to plan on starting or buying a business and simultaneously plan how you're going to sell or remove yourself from it. You may think that if starting a business is your dream, why would you want to end it? I have written this chapter to answer all of your questions. But the basic truth is, time is on your side. The longer you wait, the fewer options you might have.

Below are some benefits of establishing an exit strategy as early as possible:

Blueprint for Your Success

We all love traveling to different places. Whether you go on a family trip or a business tour, you usually have a plan for what you're going to do. You plan where you want to go ahead of time, you set meetings, and based on your destination, you prepare for your journey. Your business works the same way. When you start it, you must know where your destination is and where you want your business to go. You can also call it the vision of your business. When you are clear about the end of your journey, you are in a better position to design the framework of success. Therefore, I believe that an exit strategy is a blueprint for the success of your business. This is the part of the transferable value we have talked about throughout this book.

Strategic Decision Making

When the business owner is not clear about the vision of the business and has not crafted an exit strategy, they tend to get caught up in the day-to-day operations of the business. Being that far involved in operating the business doesn't allow them to focus on the bigger picture, of owning the business. An exit strategy helps the owner keep the endgame in view and make day-to-day decisions more strategic in nature. You often hear this as the difference between working "in" your business versus working "on" your business.

A Flexible Template

Of course, your initial exit strategy will need to be adjusted from time to time as when the situation changes. However, when you've outlined your goal from the beginning, it provides a waypoint in the future that you can use to guide your decisions when unexpected events occur. For example, a sudden death, major health problem, or a necessary relocation can cause an unexpected early departure from the business. If the exit strategy is already in place, you can quickly make any last minute adjustments to your plan without losing a tremendous amount of value.

If it's me, I try to get help from professional advisors, including a business broker, attorney, commercial real estate broker, and accountant. Working with this group will provide a solid framework for the entire business lifecycle. The business environment changes rapidly, so don't be afraid to use the pros. It will not only earn you more money in the end, it will give you peace of mind for those times when the day-to-day running of the business is so stressful.

Other Reasons to Have a Plan

As I said above that exit strategy is indeed important to sell your business. However, selling is not the only reason you should plan your end game. The following are a few reasons why you should always contemplate your exit strategy even if you have no immediate intention of selling your company.

To Avail the Benefit of an Unexpected Offer

Whether your business is small or large, the industry in which you are operating is always well aware of your performance. When your business is successful, investors may find it attractive and approach you with an intriguing offer such as merger and acquisition. If you are prepared for such an offer ahead of time, you can get the maximum benefit out of it.

To Combat Health or Family Crisis

We all know that life is unpredictable. Sudden and unexpected situations can arise at any time. We can't anticipate when these situations will occur. However, we can always be prepared in advance. A severe health issue, death of a loved one, toxic relationship, or any other problem can take your focus away from your business any time. If an exit strategy is there, you can easily take a temporary break or permanently step out of your business without having to worry about losses.

To Adjust with Economic shift

External factors such as recession may negatively impact your business. In such a situation, you may need a proper plan to adjust the operations of your business according to the need of the current economic shift. If the exit strategy is there, it will help you take the necessary steps quickly.

To Simply Have Enough Options

Even if you want to sell your business, you can't do it

overnight. You need to work on the value of your business and the potential buyers at least five to seven years before you sell your company. You have to remember that the longer you wait, or the closer you are to want to leave your business, the fewer options you will have.

Figure 13.1

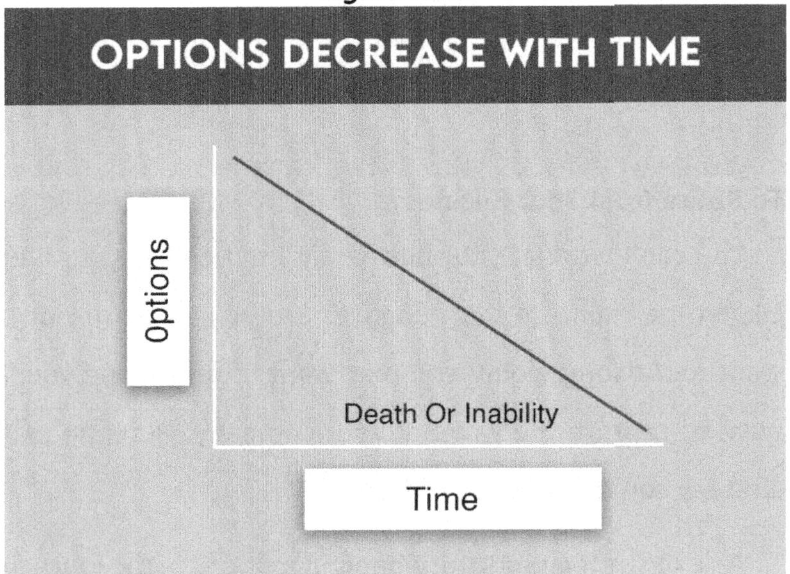

The best analogy I have heard about this reason came from Blaine Bertsch, in his book, "Pandemic Cash Flow[1]." Blaine explained that it was like standing on the side of the

[1]Bertsch, B (2020). Pandemic Cash Flow. Website. Retrieved from: http://pandemiccashflow.com/

road with a bus approaching. When you plan, it's like seeing the bus approaching from a block away. You have options. You can walk or run across the road, or just stay put on the curb. By not planning, you won't see the bus until it's right in front of you. If you mis-time your step, you could end up well, you know. You simply don't have as many options to consider if any at all. Waiting could be the worst thing you've ever done.

To Retire from Your Business

You can't work at your business till the end of your life. Ok, let me rephrase that. Chances are you won't or don't want to. At some point, you may want to retire, and you'll want to capture the value of your company. Here, an exit strategy comes for your rescue.

An exit strategy sets the wheels in motion for the journey beyond your business. Planning early gives you greater insights into your company, and the time and means to add value up until the day you decide to depart.

What Are Your Options?

There are several types of exit strategies available that successful investors and business owners consider. Among them are:

The Lifestyle Company Exit

This strategy is effective for small businesses. The business owner builds the business to enjoy a particular lifestyle. They can pocket a majority of the revenues rather than reinvesting them in the business for growth and expansion. When the business is no longer turning a profit, the owner can simply dissolve the company. However, this strategy only works when you have a good revenue stream and have partners that are on the same page as you.

The Legacy Exit

The Legacy exit is suitable when you want to keep the business in the family. This is a recommended exit strategy for those who want to transition the company to a child or other relative. However, for a successful transition, you must start working on succession planning years before the transition, which will assist in the seamless execution of your exit strategy. Through careful planning, you can exit the company with a period of annuity payments from the company, and allow your relatives to acquire the business with very little money out of their own pockets.

The M&A Exit

Mergers and acquisitions are ideal for any company. Start-up companies especially look forward to selling their controlling interest to a larger, more profitable business. In this type of exit strategy, owners remain a part of the business even after the merger. With this one, you should always make sure you trust that the acquiring company is as dedicated to the growth of your business as you are, or at least get paid handsomely to let your dream go.

The Acqui-hire Exit

Acqui-hire is an exit strategy in which a company buys out a business for the sake of acquiring its skilled employees. This type of acquisition is very beneficial to your employees, ensuring that they will be taken care of in the long run. One of the components of your succession planning is to identify the needs of the organization to make sure that your employees will benefit and thrive through the change in ownership.

The Management and/or Employee Buyout Exit

Management and employee buyout is a strategy when a business is sold to its employees, both managerial and non-managerial. This type of exit strategy helps maintain your company's legacy. This allows for more flexibility in your exit strategy. In fact, with an ESOP (Employee Stock Option Program), you can pre-plan the transition and ensure that the money for the acquisition is in place well ahead of the actual event.

The Selling Your Stake to A Partner or Investor Exit

Selling your stake is a way to keep business running as usual. It's a very common exit strategy and allows owners to simply sell off their stakes without having to make huge changes to the company. Often, you will see this as part of the Articles of Incorporation or by-laws of a company. This means that you have agreed in advance how departures will be treated and paid.

The Initial Public Offering (IPO) Exit

IPOs are the method of selling shares of stock of your privately owned business to the public. If you're looking for the most rewarding and thrilling exit strategy, IPO is your option. However, it is profitable only when it is done properly. This type of strategy brings in large amounts of cash within a short period of time, but it comes with consequences and scrutiny. Make sure your business performance will exceed the expectations of the public. Especially the external conditions around your industry. Even if your business is doing well, your industry may lack appeal to the public.

The Liquidation Exit

Liquidating is an exit strategy when you close your business and sell all of your assets, mostly at a lower cost. This is a recommended strategy when the time has come to simply move on. If you choose this route, just know that you will need to use the cash to pay your shareholders if there are any as well as eliminate any debts.

Which One Is The Best?

The best type of exit strategy depends on the type and size of your business. A partner in a medical office might benefit by selling to one of the other existing partners, while a sole proprietor's ideal exit strategy might simply be to make as much money as possible, then close down the business. If the company has multiple founders, or if there are substantial shareholders in addition to the founders, these other parties' interests must be factored into the choice of an exit strategy as well.

In the downloadable resources sections of www.cashflowmike.com, I've put a few checklists and templates to help you think through this process. No matter which exit strategy you choose for your business, you should always be clear about your financial goals. There is no one-size-fits-all business exit strategy. The exit strategy that's right for you and your business will depend on several different factors and may change or develop as you progress through the lifecycle of your business.

However, the best thing you can do concerning an exit strategy business plan is to actually plan. Even when you start your business, you should consider the possibilities around leaving your business, if something unexpected happens. If you're proactive in thinking about this process—what it might look like, how it might be executed, and what the consequences will be—you're more likely to have success when it's time to part ways.

But I don't want to leave you hanging. The best exit strategy is going to be dependent on the goals you have for the following components. You have to ask yourself some questions about what your life beyond working will look like. Do you care about your legacy? Do you want to take care of key employees? Are there investors or other parties that will be impacted? These questions will help you determine which options might fit your definition of a "great exit", meaning it does the most good. Here is a chart to help you remember to think of other items when planning your exit strategy.

Figure 13.2

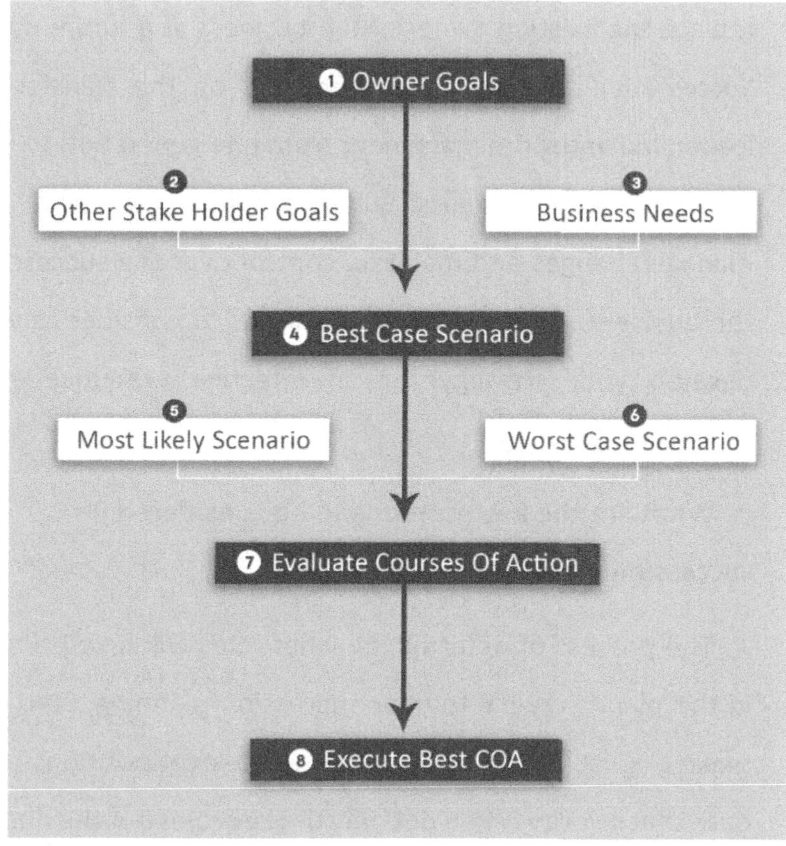

Succession Planning

If you would like the business to continue even after you're gone, you have to start working on succession planning years ahead. Succession Planning is the process of identifying successors within a business and providing them with an opportunity to develop their skills and experience to replace the existing owner of the business at a future date. Succession Planning primarily focuses on the transfer of leadership and/or management from one generation to the next within the business. Succession planning helps you manage changes and maintain control over the success of the business. Here are a few questions to consider as you develop your strategy for an effective executive-level succession plan:

What are the key positions to be considered for succession planning?

The process of determining what roles will take priority in the plan is crucial to your succession planning. Start by making a list of the priority executive-level positions and base that priority list on not only the key roles but the duties of each role and whether there are any significant "unique" skill sets held by the person currently in that role. The less you have to rely on any person's uniqueness, the better you can transition when the time comes. Meaning that, "only they can do that job", will be a liability for you in the future.

Who are your possible successors or what are the criteria for choosing those successors?

Identify the individuals currently in your organization who are prime candidates to take over leadership roles in the event of a key executive's exit. If you aren't clear about specific individuals in your organization who could take over such a vital role, then start by making a list of the key skills, training, and other criteria that anyone in that role would have to maintain.

What training programs are in place (or will you need to put into place) to properly train candidates as successors?

Now that you have become clear on the criteria for a successor in any given executive-level role in your company, it should also become more clear what training programs you have available to meet the needs of your succession plan...and also, what holes you may have in your systems now. You may need to fill the gap in your training programs to confidently move forward with your succession plan and assure that you will always have a qualified individual in line to take over the leadership reins.

Are your key executive-level processes and procedures documented?

The best way to implement a smooth transition is to create "users manuals" for key positions (ultimately, ALL positions) in addition to your training programs for key candidates. When you have your processes and procedures documented, you make it considerably easier for someone else to effectively step into a role previously held by another.

It generally takes four to six years to create an effective exit strategy and prepare the business for a profitable and smooth transition. You can't just wake up one day and decide you don't want to do it anymore. The most successful exit strategies are the ones that were planned years in advance. Frequently, they leverage one or two key factors such as profits, customer experience, supply chain, or organization. Think about an exit strategy for your business and plan ahead. You can then decide when to act.

Chapter 14
SO, WHAT'S THE POINT?

Why does someone start a business?

This is a simple question, and almost everyone who is asked this question says that everyone starts a business to earn money. Well, this answer is absolutely right, but what is the core objective behind earning a whole lot of money? Why do we need money? You might be wondering why I am asking this question. The logic is very simple. Everyone wants to earn money because they want to improve their lifestyle.

They want to enjoy a luxurious life. When a business owner starts their business, they also have a dream in their mind to upgrade their lifestyle. However, the responsibilities and duties that come with the newly established business make them so occupied that they can't maintain a balance between their personal and professional life. My idea of writing this book was to give a way to people that could help them create a lifestyle-friendly business. A business that doesn't consume their entire existence. You must have noticed that every method that I have shared in this book is very simple and straightforward. They save a lot of your time and energy. This is because I want you to utilize your time as efficiently as possible.

So, by now, you know what to do to avoid being a D.U.M.B. business owner. Your purpose is not to be a good business owner only. You have to strive to be more than just good at your trade. You have to see the business through the eyes of the financial statements. Not only that, but you also have to be able to have confidence in taking corrective action when an issue begins to surface. Bad news does not get better with time, you have to change the dynamics of your business as you identify issues.

Let's take a look back at the concepts you learned in this book, and give you a place of reference to revisit the material as you encounter these cash critical situations.

1. Start with the end in mind: When you start a business, you must know why you are starting it. If you are going to spend time in your business, you have to know your WHY? Maybe you want to do it because you want money or simply because doing business is your passion. Whatever your WHY is, you must be sure where do you see yourself at the end of this business. Understanding what you want your exit to look like will help you make the right decisions regularly.

2. The Home Run Financial System: To accurately measure your company, you need a methodology to assess its health. The Home Run Financial System is a way to look at all three financial statements in less than seven minutes per month. It's a simple yet in-depth analysis of the health of your business. It gives you a clear picture of where you stand currently.

3. Mine Your Business for Hidden Cash: Once you get to know about the health of your business, the next step is to treat any issues that are affecting the health of your business negatively. At this stage, we use the Financial Doctor Method of financial ratio analysis to look for inefficiencies in your current business operation. You can compare yourself to the industry average or any other metric that you measure your business against

4. The Fast Money Formula: One of the most critical things that business owners fail to actively manage is their cash conversion cycle. The speed that cash moves through the company are what keeps the business alive. Your goal is to reduce the size of your cash gap. That way, you will ultimately need less money to run your business.

5. Forecasting by The Numbers: Sometimes, you don't know that your business has more capacity than it currently runs at. Your underutilized skills keep your business from operating at its full capacity. These underutilized skills are a way to save your business. If a business owner understands what they can achieve, they are more likely to accomplish it. Take the time to match your vision of the future with the reality of how your business works to maximize the amount of cash you have in your business

6. How to Deal with Your Banker: Like it or not, we need the banker to grow our businesses. The real problem arises when the two parties don't talk to each other in a way they both can understand. Your role as a business owner is to arm the banker with enough of the RIGHT information, so they can advocate for you in a loan committee and be your quarterback to understanding all of the ways your bank can help you. For this purpose, you have to be well-informed and enlightened about your business in the first place. You and your banker can be on the same page only when you know your business.

7. The Simple Valuation Formula: Let's face it. Your small business might be one of the largest investments you have made in your life. A lot of your future depends on your ability to run the business profitably and exit the company with the amount you need to fund your transferable value dream. Knowing the value of your company helps you determine if you are on the right track when it comes to your exit.

8. The Deliberate Exit Plan: If you start with the end in mind, you are already thinking about what your future beyond the company will look like. Exiting your company is a planned event that you want to be in control of. By planning early and often, you give yourself the best chance to exit on your terms and at your price.

What Makes Your Business Successful?

Success is a subjective term. Its meaning varies from person to person. What makes business success depends on how you define this concept in the first place; people perceive success quite differently. As Richard Branson says,

"Too many people measure how successful they are by how much money they make or the people that they associate with. In my opinion, true success should be measured by how happy you are."

You can have a small business that provides steady revenue and see it as a success. Or you can run a multi-million-dollar company and feel that you're not "doing enough."

If you want to become a successful business owner, know what your vision is. What transferable value you want to build. Where you see yourself at the end of your business. If thinking about all these things fires you up and gives you motivation, know that you are on the right path. My dream for you is to build a lifestyle-friendly business. One that supports your current lifestyle and the one you dream about in the future. It is important to be aware from the outset that there is no magic bullet that can transform you into a rich and successful entrepreneur overnight. However, for those prepared to work hard to succeed, there is an almost formulaic blend of entrepreneurial skills that can help set successful business owners apart from the rest. Remember, money is not the dream. It is a way to fund it, so you have to focus on the accumulation of wealth as a critical business function every day you go to work.

The Clear Path to Cash will help you make great decisions at the right time, but you have to execute. No method works if you don't fully embrace it and make it a part of your business fabric. So, wrap yourself in the comfort of cash flow and see how your life changes. Thanks for being a part of my dream of helping small business owners. My last piece of advice to you is simple: Don't Be a D.U.M.B. Business Owner.

Clear PATH To Cash
More Money, More Time, Better Business

Made in the USA
Middletown, DE
23 September 2022

11060480R00166